VALUABLE
LINCOLN PENNY ERROR COIN
HANDBOOK

JASON WHITMORE

Copyright © 2024 by Jason Whitmore - All rights reserved.

No portion of this book may be reproduced in any form without written permission from the publisher or author, except as permitted by U.S. copyright law.

This publication is designed to provide accurate and authoritative information in regard to the subject matter covered. It is sold with the understanding that neither the author nor the publisher is engaged in rendering legal, investment, accounting or other professional services. While the publisher and author have used their best efforts in preparing this book, they make no representations or warranties with respect to the accuracy or completeness of the contents of this book and specifically disclaim any implied warranties of merchantability or fitness for a particular purpose. No warranty may be created or extended by sales representatives or written sales materials. The advice and strategies contained herein may not be suitable for your situation. You should consult with a professional when appropriate. Neither the publisher nor the author shall be liable for any loss of profit or any other commercial damages, including but not limited to special, incidental, consequential, personal, or other damages.

CONTENTS

Introduction	1
1. History and Evolution of the Lincoln Penny	3
Origins of the Lincoln Penny	4
Key Design Changes	5
Minting Process and Error Origins	8
2. Understanding Error Coins and Varieties	11
Defining Error Coins and Varieties	12
Types of Coin Errors	13
Die Errors	13
Planchet Errors	14
Strike Errors	15
Hub Errors	15
Importance of Error Coins in Collecting	18
Common Misconceptions About Error Coins	19
3. Identifying Lincoln Penny Errors	21
Essential Tools for Error Identification	22
Step-by-Step Guide to Examining Pennies	23
Common Lincoln Penny Errors	24
4. Mastering Authentication Techniques	29
Distinguishing Genuine Errors from Altered Coins	30

Microscopic Examination Techniques	31
Red Flags for Counterfeit Error Coins	32
Abnormalities in Edge	33
Magnetic Properties	34
Die Characteristics	35
Using Technology In Authentication	36
Weight and Measurement Tools	37
When To Seek Professional Authentication	38
The Authentication Process	39
Cost Benefit Analysis	39
5. Grading and Valuing Error Coins	**43**
Understanding Grading Codes for E rror Coins	44
Understanding The Error Grading Scale	52
Specific Grading Considerations	53
Factors Affecting The Value of Error Coins	55
Rarity	55
Historical Significance	56
Condition and Grade	56
Visual Appeal	56
Market Trends and Demand	57
Price Guides and Resources For Valuation	57
Print Resources	57
Online Auction Archives	57
Market Analysis Websites	58
Independent Market Resources	58
How To Interpret and Use Price Guides Effectively	58
Published Prices vs. Real Market	59
Time-Based Analysis	59
Population Impact	59
Condition Specifics	59
Market Context	59
Authentication Status	60
Getting Coins Professionally Graded	60
Professional Certification Services (PCGS)	60
Numismatic Guaranty Corporation (NGC)	60
American Numismatic Association Certification Service (ANACS)	61

Deciding When to Grade	61
Service Selection Factors	61
The Submission Process	61

6. Building Your Lincoln Penny Error Collection — 65

Developing a Collecting Strategy	66
Balancing Rarity, Condition, and Budget	67
Strategies for Upgrading Your Collection Over Time	68
Where To Find Errors	69
Coin Roll Hunting	71
Local Coin Shops and Dealers	71
Online Marketplaces	71
Coin Shows and Conventions	72
Social Media and Online Communities	72
Coin Roll Hunting Techniques	73
Proper Etiquette	74
Record-Keeping Systems	75
Realistic Expectations	76
Attending Coin Shows and Auctions	76
Building Relationships With Dealers and Collectors	77

7. Preserving and Displaying Your Collection — 79

Proper Handling Techniques	80
Tools For Proper Coin Manipulation	81
Storage Options and Best Practices	82

8. The Market For Lincoln Penny Errors — 85

Current Trends In The Error Coin Market	86
Places To Sell Your Coins	87
Online Marketplaces	87
Heritage Auctions and Great Collections	87
Face-to-Face Sales at Shows	88
Local Coin Shop Relationships	88
Specialty Forums and Websites	88
Traditional Auction Houses	88
Tips for Buying and Selling Online	89
Creating Effective Listings	89
Payment Methods and Shipping	91
Red Flags in Online Transactions	93

Building a Reputation as a Collector or Dealer	94
Sharing Knowledge and Contributing to the Community	96
Handling Disputes Properly	97
Conclusion	**99**
References	**101**

A BONUS FOR YOU

Before you start your collecting journey, download our comprehensive guide:

The Essential Coin Collector's Glossary: *Your Go-To Guide for Rare and Valuable Coins. A Complete Glossary of Valuable Coins, Lincoln Pennies, and U.S. Error Coins with Names and Descriptions for Aspiring Collectors.*

This invaluable resource provides a complete glossary of terms covering valuable coins, Lincoln cents, and U.S. error coins—knowledge that will help you build and develop your collection with confidence.

Inside this free guide, you'll discover:

- Clear definitions of essential collecting terms
- Specific terminology for Lincoln cent collecting
- Detailed error coin vocabulary
- Advanced collecting and grading terms
- Professional dealer language

Simply scan the QR code below to access your free copy. Consider it your personal dictionary for the fascinating world of coin collecting.

INTRODUCTION

Coin collecting started with my grandfather. That's how I developed my passion for it. Without fail, on Sundays, he'd call me into his study—a warm, wood-paneled room that smelled of pipe tobacco and history and there, at his heavy oak desk, he'd pull out his treasured coin albums, each one carefully cataloged and annotated in his precise handwriting.

"The real value isn't just in the metal," he'd say, holding up a wheat penny to the light streaming through his window. "It's in the stories these coins tell us—about our country, about the people who made them, and sometimes, about the mistakes that make certain coins extraordinary."

I didn't know then that those Sunday afternoon lessons would lead me to become one of the foremost specialists in Lincoln penny errors, with over three decades of experience in authentication and valuation. What started as a boy watching his grandfather examine coins through a jeweler's loupe has evolved into a lifelong quest to understand and document every significant Lincoln penny variation and error.

In this book, I'm sharing what I've learned from examining thousands of specimens, dealing with countless collectors, and, yes, occasionally falling prey to clever counterfeits in my early days. You'll learn to distinguish genuine errors from altered coins, understand the market forces that drive valuations, and develop the expertise to spot promising specimens that others might overlook. I've also included high-resolution images, each carefully selected to illustrate specific characteristics that can mean the difference between a common cent and a four-figure rarity.

My grandfather passed away twenty years ago, but I still hear his voice when I'm examining a doubled die or an off-center strike. "Take your time," he'd say. "The story's in the details." This book is my way of passing on that legacy—not just the technical knowledge of what makes an error coin valuable, but the pure joy of discovery that comes with each new find. I hope it helps you avoid the pitfalls I've encountered and leads you to some treasures of your own.

1

HISTORY AND EVOLUTION OF THE LINCOLN PENNY

The first book that I got about Lincoln Cent wasn't even about errors—it was a worn Whitman folder I found at a flea market for fifty cents. The blue cardboard was dog-eared, and someone had already filled the 1941-1958 slots. But that empty space for the 1909 VDB captured my imagination like nothing else. I remember asking my grandfather why that particular penny was so special, and his answer launched me into a fascinating journey through American history.

The Lincoln Cent stands as a milestone in American coinage. It marked the first appearance of a president's portrait on a circulating U.S. coin, boldly departing from the traditional allegorical Liberty figure that had appeared on cents since 1793. President Theodore Roosevelt championed this artistic advancement, envisioning coins that would showcase both American excellence and honor our greatest citizens.

Victor David Brenner's 1909 design has proven enduring—the longest-running design on any circulating coin in U.S. history. The penny's evolution tells a remarkable story through its changing production methods, metallic content, and role in commerce. Each of these transformations opened the door for fascinating errors, making the Lincoln Cent series one of the most exciting areas for collectors to explore.

ORIGINS OF THE LINCOLN PENNY

The birth of the Lincoln Cent in 1909 marked a triumphant moment in American numismatic history. President Theodore Roosevelt, who was a passionate advocate for beautiful American coinage, saw an opportunity to commemorate the 100th anniversary of Abraham Lincoln's birth with a stunning new design. His vision extended beyond mere currency—he sought to create pocket-sized works of art that Americans would carry proudly.

The selection of Victor David Brenner as the coin's designer proved inspiring. A Lithuanian immigrant who had risen to prominence as one of America's finest medallists, Brenner brought deep artistic sensitivity to the project. His Lincoln portrait captured the president's strength and dignity, drawing inspiration from a photograph taken by Civil War photographer Mathew Brady. The design featured Lincoln's noble profile on the obverse, while two elegant wheat stalks framed the reverse—symbols of America's agricultural abundance.

The initial release of the Lincoln cent on August 2, 1909, sparked unprecedented public excitement. Banks across the country saw lines forming as Americans eagerly sought to obtain these remarkable new coins. The Philadelphia Mint produced 27,995,000 pieces in just the first few days, yet still struggled to meet public demand.

The coin's design included Brenner's initials—VDB—prominently placed on the reverse. This artistic signature sparked spirited discussion in the press, leading the Mint to modify the design. The VDB cents released before this change became instant collectors' items, cherished by numismatists to this day.

Within weeks, the Lincoln Cent achieved widespread acceptance, earning praise for its artistic merit and historical significance. The public embraced this revolutionary change in American coinage, setting the stage for numismatic innovation. Brenner's masterful design would go on to inspire generations of coin collectors while establishing a new standard for American monetary art.

Key Design Changes

The Lincoln Cent's evolution tells an inspiring story of American artistry and innovation through its distinctive reverse designs. The original Wheat ears design (1909-1958) set a standard for elegance with its simple yet graceful composition. For half a century, these "Wheaties" circulated widely, becoming beloved symbols of American commerce and a cornerstone of countless collections.

1959 ushered in a magnificent transformation as the Lincoln Memorial replaced the Wheat Stalk's reverse. This intricate design by Frank Gasparro paid tribute to both Lincoln and American architecture, with the president's statue visible between the Memorial's columns. The detail proved so precise that keen-eyed collectors could even spot the statue on well-preserved specimens.

The most dramatic design evolution came during World War II when the Mint adapted brilliantly to wartime copper shortages. The 1943 zinc-coated steel cents shimmered with a unique silver appearance, standing apart as the only circulating U.S. coin made from steel. The Mint returned to a modified bronze composition in 1944, creating fascinating opportunities for collectors to discover transitional composition errors.

Lincoln's bicentennial in 2009 brought an unprecedented celebration of design creativity. The Mint released four stunning reverse designs chronicling Lincoln's life journey:

- His Kentucky birth cabin, rendered in rustic detail
- His formative years in Indiana, showing young Lincoln reading
- His professional life in Illinois, depicting him at the state capitol
- The partially constructed Capitol dome, representing his presidency

In 2010, the Union Shield reverse emerged as a powerful symbol of national unity. This bold design by Lyndall Bass features the thirteen stripes of the shield topped by the E PLURIBUS UNUM banner, creating clean lines that showcase mint characteristics clearly.

Each design transition has opened exciting possibilities for error collectors. The changing relief, intricate details, and evolving strike requirements have produced remarkable varieties. Hub changes, die states, and composition transitions offer collectors a rich field for discovery. Modern Shield cents continue this tradition, with their precise design elements making doubled dies and other striking errors particularly distinctive.

These evolutionary steps have made the Lincoln Cent series one of the most rewarding for error collectors. Every design change brings unique characteristics that help us authenticate and classify errors more accurately, adding depth and value to our collecting experience.

Minting Process and Error Origins

The creation of a Lincoln cent showcases American engineering at its finest, combining precision machinery with time-honored techniques. Modern minting begins with huge copper sheets fed through blanking machines, which punch out perfect circles called planchets. These gleaming blank discs then embark on a remarkable journey through the Mint's production floor.

The planchets first dance through an annealing furnace, where carefully controlled heat softens the metal to accept crisp designs. A bath in brightening solution follows, giving each blank its characteristic shine. The upturned rim, vital for protecting the coin's design, takes shape as the blanks spin through the upsetting mill.

The heart of minting magic happens at the coining press, where immense pressure transforms plain planchets into works of art. Modern presses strike up to 750 coins per minute, applying tons of pressure to imprint Lincoln's portrait and the reverse design. This incredible speed and force create opportunities for fascinating errors:

- Die cracks can develop as the hardy steel dies meet thousands of planchets

- Multiple strikes sometimes occur when planchets linger in the press

- Off-center strikes emerge when planchets drift from their precise position

- Die deterioration produces progressive stages of interesting varieties

Each U.S. Mint facility brings its own character to penny production:

- Philadelphia (no mint mark) leads innovation in minting technology
- Denver (D) produces billions of cents annually for Western states
- San Francisco (S) specialized in proof cents until 1975
- West Point (W) creates special collector editions

The evolution of minting technology tells an exciting story of continuous improvement. The transition from screw presses to steam-powered equipment, and finally to modern electronic striking machines, has created distinctive patterns of errors unique to each era. Early mechanical presses often produced doubled dies, while today's high-speed equipment can generate fascinating die varieties and striking anomalies.

Modern quality control catches most errors, making those that escape even more prized by collectors. Digital scanning equipment monitors die wear and striking pressure, but the complex dance of metal and machinery still produces remarkable variations. Each advancement in minting technology opens doors to new categories of errors, giving collectors fresh territory to explore.

2

UNDERSTANDING ERROR COINS AND VARIETIES

The vault at Heritage Auction s fell silent as the auctioneer lifted the 1969-S doubled die cent. Five seconds later, the room erupted in a bidding frenzy that would push the final price to over $120,000. What made this small copper disc so valuable? A microscopic misalignment in the hubbing process—a mistake that transformed an ordinary penny into numismatic gold.

Error coins challenge our perception of perfection. In a world where modern minting technology strives for flawless reproduction, these remind us that uniqueness often carries more value than precision. A shifted die, a displaced planchet, or a metal mixing mishap can create something extraordinary from the ordinary.

This chapter will help you understand more clearly why a seemingly pristine penny might be worth a few cents, while one that appears "imperfect" could fund a college education. The key lies in understanding not just what makes an error, but why these variations occur and which ones matter most to collectors.

DEFINING ERROR COINS AND VARIETIES

Error coins and varieties represent two distinct branches of numismatic study, each telling its own story about the minting process. Mint errors emerge from momentary disruptions in production—planchets feeding incorrectly, dies clashing together, or metal flows behaving unpredictably. These unique pieces capture specific instances when standard minting operations took an unexpected turn.

Varieties, by contrast, come from different sources. They arise when dies undergo modifications, show progressive wear patterns, or receive multiple impressions during the hubbing process. While every 1955 doubled die cent displays identical characteristics, each off-center strike tells its own unique tale.

The U.S. Mint maintains strict protocols for handling production anomalies:

- Quality control teams intercept and destroy most error pieces
- Some categories, like minor die varieties, receive approval for release
- Major errors trigger immediate production line inspections
- Statistical tracking helps identify concerning patterns

Distinguishing mint-made errors from post-mint damage requires careful analysis:

Mint-Made Characteristics:

- Metal flow patterns match the moment of striking
- Design elements show consistent displacement
- Surface texture aligns with production methods
- Die characteristics remain visible despite the error

Post-Mint Damage Indicators:

- Metal displacement conflicts with striking patterns
- Tool marks or artificial alterations appear
- Surface texture shows environmental exposure
- Design elements exhibit unnatural distortion

Professional grading services are key in authentication, employing advanced imaging technology alongside traditional examination methods. Their expertise helps protect collectors from artificial alterations and provides standardized descriptions for various error types.

TYPES OF COIN ERRORS

At the Philadelphia Mint, exactly 850 tons of pressure transform each blank planchet into a Lincoln cent. This massive force, applied for a fraction of a second, must align perfectly with dies, collar, and metal to create a standard penny. When any element shifts from this precision dance, errors emerge. Each variation—from subtle to spectacular—maps to a specific moment in the minting process, leaving distinct evidence of its creation.

Modern minting produces billions of coins annually, yet even the most sophisticated machinery cannot eliminate every possible error. Understanding how and where these variations occur transforms collecting from simple accumulation into strategic pursuit. Here's how to recognize and classify the major categories of mint errors that appear in Lincoln cents.

Die Errors

When dies tell fascinating stories, collectors listen. Doubled dies create spectacular visual effects, like the legendary 1955 DDO where every letter and number appears to dance with its shadow. Repunched mint marks showcase tiny but significant shifts, such as the 1944 D/S where Denver's mark boldly overlays San Francisco's initial punch. Die cracks develop character as strikes continue—the 1956 "Line in Lincoln's Forehead" variety demonstrates how these flaws evolve into prized collectibles.

Planchet Errors

Raw material anomalies produce some of the numismatics' most intriguing pieces. The 1943 bronze cent stands as the ultimate wrong planchet error, created when copper planchets lingered in the feed tubes during wartime steel production. Clipped planchets display distinctive characteristics—curved clips follow the circular punch pattern, while straight clips reveal challenges in strip alignment. The 1982 transition from copper to zinc opened fresh opportunities for transitional errors.

Strike Errors

Off-center strikes range from subtle to dramatic—a 1950-D struck 50% off-center commands attention in any collection. Multiple strikes tell complex tales: a 1995 penny struck three times and rotated between strikes, creating a mesmerizing spiral effect. Broadstrikes burst beyond their intended boundaries when collar dies malfunction, allowing the metal to flow unrestricted.

Hub Errors

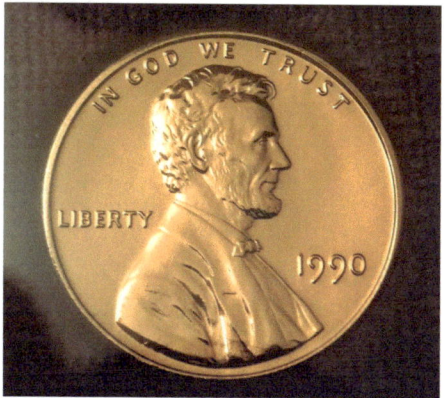

Hub errors reshape familiar designs in unexpected ways. The 1990 "No S" proof cent demonstrates complete design element omission. Misaligned hubbing creates subtle shifts in detail placement—the 1960 "Small Date" variety emerged from this process. Modern computerized hubbing reduces these variations, making classic hub errors increasingly desirable.

Notable Lincoln Cent Examples:

- 1922 "Plain"—No D mint mark due to die polishing

- 1958 "Doubled Die Reverse"—Sharp doubling on wheat ears

- 1969-S "Doubled Die Obverse"—One of the most valuable modern errors

VALUABLE LINCOLN PENNY ERROR COIN HANDBOOK

- 1983 "Doubled Die Reverse"—Shows strong doubling on STATES

- 1984 "Doubled Ear"—Extra ear detail creates an optical illusion

Each error type reveals unique characteristics under magnification:
- Die errors show raised, mirror-image doubling
- Planchet errors display distinctive metal flow patterns
- Strike errors create sharp outline demarcations
- Hub errors maintain consistent characteristics across multiple dies

IMPORTANCE OF ERROR COINS IN COLLECTING

Market data tells a compelling story: while a standard 1969-S Lincoln cent trades for a few dollars, the doubled die variety commands six figures at auction. This stark value difference illustrates why error coins captivate serious collectors. Each error represents a unique moment in production—a snapshot frozen in metal that can never be exactly duplicated.

Error coins transform collecting dynamics in several key ways:

Rarity Factors

- Production errors face multiple elimination points
- Quality control typically catches major variations
- Few specimens survive mint detection systems
- Each category has its own survival rate pattern
- Many major errors exist in quantities under 100 pieces

Value Dynamics

- Market appreciation often outpaces standard issues
- Certain errors appreciate independently of grade
- Discovery of new examples rarely impacts established prices
- Type collectors seek representative errors
- Condition plays a unique role in error evaluation

Research Significance

- Error coins document minting technology evolution
- Each major error advances the understanding of production methods
- Specialists study error patterns to decode mint operations
- New discoveries still emerge from older issues
- Error analysis helps authenticate regular issues

Beyond traditional collecting metrics, error coins offer insight into industrial processes. A doubled die reveals the mechanics of die preparation. An off-center strike demonstrates planchet feeding systems. A wrong planchet error maps material handling procedures. This technical dimension adds depth to the collecting strategy.

The growing sophistication of authentication tools has strengthened the error market. Advanced imaging technology confirms genuine errors while exposing alterations; this technical validation builds collector confidence and supports market stability.

Common Misconceptions About Error Coins

A seasoned dealer at the ANA World's Fair of Money spread out a dozen "error" cents on his velvet display pad. "Which ones catch your eye?" he asked visitors. Most picked the most damaged pieces while walking past a subtle but valuable doubled die. This simple demonstration reveals how misconceptions shape the error coin market.

The gap between perception and reality is what often leads enthusiasts astray. Many beginners mistake post-mint damage for valuable errors, drawn to dramatic scratches or environmental effects rather than authentic mint-made variations. A bent coin might look unusual, but the natural metal flow patterns present in genuine errors tell a different story. Understanding these patterns transforms how we evaluate potential acquisitions.

Market expectations pose another challenge. Yes, those stories of five-figure error sales inspire treasure hunts through pocket change, but most off-center strikes trade for modest premiums. The key lies in understanding rarity within specific error categories; while thousands of minor die cracks exist, only a handful of dramatic doubled dies have survived quality control measures.

Artificial errors present a sophisticated challenge. Modern tools can simulate mint errors with increasing skill, however, these pieces lack crucial characteristics. Genuine errors display specific metal flow patterns that align with known manufacturing steps. Professional authentication has become essential, especially for significant purchases.

The quest for the "perfect" coin leads some collectors down an unrealistic path. Every coin, even those appearing flawless, carries microscopic variations from the ideal design. Modern minting achieves remarkable precision, but understanding normal production variance helps distinguish genuine errors from standard acceptable ranges.

Authentication services play a crucial role, combining advanced analysis tools with traditional expertise. Their findings protect collectors and support market stability, helping separate genuine prizes from altered pieces.

3

IDENTIFYING LINCOLN PENNY ERRORS

The electron microscope reveals a landscape of ridges and valleys across the Lincoln cent's surface. At 500x magnification, even "normal" coins display subtle variations. At 2000x, genuine errors tell their stories through distinctive metal flow patterns and crystalline structures. While most collectors will never examine their coins at this level, understanding how professionals authenticate errors transforms how we view every penny in our collection.

These microscopic details matter because they form the foundation of error authentication. Metal flows like a liquid under the tremendous pressure of the minting press, creating distinctive patterns unique to each type of error. A genuine doubled die shows specific crystalline arrangements where the design elements overlap. Strike errors display characteristic metal displacement that no tool can perfectly replicate.

Professional authenticators combine this scientific understanding with decades of practical experience. Their tools range from simple magnification to sophisticated imaging technology, each revealing different aspects of a coin's surface. This systematic approach to error identification has revolutionized collecting, turning gut feelings into measurable characteristics.

For the dedicated collector, this scientific foundation translates into practical skills. A basic 10x loupe reveals enough detail to begin identifying major error categories. With practice, you'll spot the telltale signs that distinguish genuine errors from damage or alteration; the following sections will guide you through this identification process, from basic diagnostics to advanced authentication techniques.

ESSENTIAL TOOLS FOR ERROR IDENTIFICATION

Proper magnification sets the foundation for discovery. Start with a quality 10x loupe—this is your primary tool, revealing sufficient detail for most initial assessments. When you're ready to advance, add a 16x or 20x loupe to your kit. Be wary of higher magnifications; they often sacrifice clarity for power. The quality of the glass matters more than maximum magnification, so invest in coated lenses that minimize distortion.

Lighting takes out all the guesswork and turns it into science. A flexible desk lamp with daylight-balanced LED bulbs provides even illumination without harsh shadows. You'll need to position your light source at a 45-degree angle to the coin's surface to reveal raised elements and distinct patterns. This setup helps identify genuine doubled dies and authenticate strike errors.

Digital microscopes have also revolutionized error authentication. Modern USB microscopes capture high-resolution images at 20x to 200x magnification, perfect for documenting discoveries and seeking expert opinions. These images prove invaluable when comparing questionable pieces against verified examples or sharing finds with other collectors.

Your success rate demands reliable reference data. You must build your knowledge base through specialized guides focusing on Lincoln Cent errors. Online resources like CONECA's error-variety attribution files provide current market insights and discovery reports. The most valuable reference often comes from handling verified examples at major coin shows.

Precise measurements bring certainty to identification. Digital calipers accurate to 0.01mm help verify planchet specifications and document strike characteristics. A quality gram scale confirms proper weight ranges for composition errors. Consider adding a digital angle gauge for measuring rotated die errors and a high-quality LED flashlight for portable examination.

Quality tools lead to confident attributions. Each instrument plays a specific role in the examination process, working together to verify the authenticity of your potential error coin.

I inherited a beautiful mahogany desk from my mentor, Paul Evans, after his passing in 2018. Inside one drawer, there was one of his original coin examination kits from the 1960s—a scratched brass loupe, a handheld scale that had seen better days, and a stack of dog-eared reference books. While those tools helped him discover some legendary error varieties, including an unlisted 1960 doubled die cent, they pale in comparison to what we have available today, however, every time I plug in my digital microscope or check CONECA's online archives, I think about him squinting through that old loupe, making groundbreaking discoveries with basic tools and determination. The fundamentals haven't changed, but our ability to detect, document, and share our findings has evolved dramatically. Good tools don't make the collector, but they sure make the journey more rewarding.

Step-by-Step Guide to Examining Pennies

My first major error finding ended up being a fingerprint-smudged disappointment. After hours of excitement over what I thought was a 1972 double die, I rushed it to a dealer at the Memphis Money Show without even cleaning my hands after lunch. Pulling out his loupe, he visibly winced at the fresh smudges across the surface. "This is a genuine doubled die," he confirmed, "but those fingerprints just cut its value in half." That $900 lesson—the difference between what I could have gotten and what I did get—transformed how I approach every potential error coin. Now, twenty years later, I still have that same coin in my reference collection, its smudged surface serving as a permanent reminder that proper handling techniques aren't just suggestions—they're essential steps that can make or break a coin's value.

You have to understand that the examination commences right before you touch the piece. Create a clean workspace with a soft cloth surface. Cotton gloves protect valuable specimens, though bare hands work fine for initial sorting if they're clean and dry. Hold coins by their edges, letting light play across the surface to reveal potential areas of interest.

Start your inspection with a broad view. Hold the coin eight inches from your eyes under good lighting. Rotate it slowly, watching how light reveals the overall surface character. This initial scan often reveals striking errors or major die varieties. Many significant errors announce themselves at this stage through unusual shapes or dramatic design elements.

The obverse deserves careful attention under magnification. Focus first on Lincoln's portrait—particularly the hair, ear, and coat details where doubled dies often show their strongest features. Watch for unusual metal flow around letters and numbers. DATE and LIBERTY merit special scrutiny as prime areas for variety hunting.

Moving to the reverse, examine each letter of E PLURIBUS UNUM individually. The shield's vertical lines provide natural measuring posts for alignment errors. The lettering of ONE CENT often catches and holds evidence of die deterioration. Edge inspection requires rotating the coin under steady light, revealing clips, strike errors, or unexpected planchet problems.

Photography helps document discoveries and seek expert opinions. Position your coin flat under consistent lighting. Shoot straight down for basic documentation, then add angled shots to capture raised elements. Focus stacking software combines multiple images for sharp detail across the entire surface.

Keep in mind that the authentication will build itself from evidence, so document unusual characteristics methodically. Compare findings against verified examples. Professional certification provides final validation for significant discoveries.

Common Lincoln Penny Errors

At a recent Long Beach Expo, a young collector rushed to my table clutching a 1955 cent. "I found it in my dad's change jar!" she exclaimed. Her enthusiasm dampened when magnification revealed machine doubling rather than the coveted doubled die. Within minutes, though, she did find a legitimate die crack in another coin from the same jar—proof that understanding error varieties transforms every handful of coins into potential treasures.

Success in error collecting results from an ability to recognize the key varieties that drive the market because while hundreds of different Lincoln cent errors exist, certain types consistently command collector attention and strong premiums. The most valuable Lincoln Cent errors often appear subtle at first glance. The 1955 doubled die obverse, worth thousands today, shows its doubling most clearly in the letters and numbers. Under proper lighting, the design elements appear to step outward, creating a distinctive shelf-like appearance in LIBERTY and the date. This specific pattern helps distinguish genuine doubled dies from common machine doubling.

Off-center strikes range from minor to dramatic. A 5% shift might go unnoticed in circulation, while a 50% off-center strike immediately catches the eye. Collectors prize examples showing significant displacement while retaining a full date. The most desirable pieces display 20% to 50% off-center strikes, offering the perfect balance of error and identification.

Repunched mint marks reward patient observation. The 1944 D/S presents clear evidence of die correction—Denver's D struck over a partially effaced San Francisco mint mark. Most RPMs require magnification to spot the subtle shifts in position, size, or orientation that make them collectible.

Wrong planchet errors occur when cents are struck on planchets intended for other denominations. The difference becomes immediately apparent—a cent struck on a dime planchet appears smaller and silvery. The famous 1943 bronze cents were created when a few copper planchets from 1942 were struck instead of the intended steel ones, creating some of the most valuable Lincoln cent errors.

Die breaks start as hairline cracks and can develop into major varieties. As the die deteriorates, these breaks expand, sometimes creating raised lines across design elements. In advanced stages, pieces of the die edge can break away, forming distinctive cuds—raised, blank areas that interrupt the design. The 1922 "Plain" cent emerged when die deterioration completely removed the D mint mark.

If you have the opportunity, you should attend major coin shows and use the knowledge from this chapter to consolidate what you've learned. Watch seasoned dealers examine collections. Notice how they tilt coins at precise angles under their lights, checking specific areas for die characteristics. While books and photos help build foundational knowledge, there's no substitute for handling authenticated examples and learning from experienced collectors. The next great Lincoln cent error discovery might be sitting in your change jar or local dealer's box—but only if you know exactly what to look for and how to look for it.

4

MASTERING AUTHENTICATION TECHNIQUES

The dealer placed two 1972 doubled dies on the counter—one genuine, one altered. "Three thousand for this one," he said, pointing to the left coin. "Three dollars for the other." To the untrained eye, they looked identical. The difference? Authentic mint-made doubling leaves specific markers that no craftsman, no matter how skilled, can replicate.

I watched as other collectors examined both pieces throughout the day. Most gravitated toward the altered coin, drawn in by its more dramatic appearance. The genuine doubled die showed subtler doubling—the kind that comes from a specific hub and die misalignment during production. The altered piece displayed the tell-tale signs of mechanical manipulation, visible only to those who knew exactly where and how to look.

By day's end, three different people had tried to buy the altered coin, convinced they'd spotted an incredible bargain. Each time, the dealer turned the sale into a teaching moment. He'd pull out his fluorescent light, point out the distinctive characteristics of genuine hub doubling, and explain why the dramatic look of the altered piece actually proved its undoing. Understanding these subtle differences doesn't just prevent costly mistakes—it transforms how you evaluate every coin you encounter.

DISTINGUISHING GENUINE ERRORS FROM ALTERED COINS

Last October, a collection of "error" cents arrived at my office in a neat blue folder. Each coin had been carefully labeled: "1955 Doubled Die," "1937-D Three-Legged Buffalo," "1922 No D." The seller wanted $45,000. Within ten minutes of examination, using just a loupe and proper lighting, every piece proved artificial. The 1955 showed tooling marks in Lincoln's hair. The Buffalo's leg had been ground away rather than weakly struck. The 1922's mint mark had been deliberately removed. That folder now serves as my teaching reference—a $45,000 lesson that cost me nothing but time because I knew where to look.

Genuine mint errors carry distinctive birthmarks from their creation. Machine doubling, the most common natural variation, appears flat and shelf-like, while artificial doubling shows raised tool marks and unnatural metal flow. Authentic die deterioration creates smooth, graduated wear patterns. In contrast, intentionally removed design elements leave microscopic parallel lines or unusual depressions in the metal's surface.

Here's what artificial alterations typically reveal:

- Parallel scratch patterns from abrasive tools
- Unnatural metal displacement around design elements
- Inconsistent surface texture in modified areas
- Chemical residue in recessed areas
- Evidence of heat modification along edges
- Unusual wear patterns that don't match the coin's overall condition

Genuine mint errors show these characteristics:

- Consistent metal flow patterns
- Natural progression of die-wear
- Even surface texture across similar areas
- Expected metal displacement under magnification

- Die characteristics visible in struck portions
- Mechanical doubling that follows predictable patterns

The advent of high-speed rotary tools and sophisticated modification techniques has made authentication increasingly challenging. Modern alterations can be remarkably convincing under casual inspection. However, metal always tells the truth about how it was manipulated—if you understand what you're seeing.

Microscopic Examination Techniques

I have had to learn that experience can blind you to obvious signs. After thirty years of examining error coins, I once missed clear alteration marks on what appeared to be a doubled die because I was so excited by its potential value. Only when my colleague pointed out the subtle parallel lines in Lincoln's bowtie did I see past my own assumptions. That humbling moment taught me to approach every coin with fresh eyes and systematic scrutiny, no matter how promising it initially appears.

Surface texture analysis begins with understanding how metal behaves under minting pressure. Genuine struck surfaces display a characteristic flow pattern visible under 20x magnification. The tremendous force of the strike—over 160 tons per square inch—creates distinctive crystal patterns in the metal. These patterns remain consistent across the coin's surface, interrupted only by design elements. Any deviation from this natural flow serves as a warning sign.

When examining a coin's surface, start with low magnification and good lighting. Hold the coin at a 45-degree angle under a strong light source, slowly rotating it to reveal inconsistencies. Genuine mint errors maintain uniform luster within similar surfaces. Altered areas interrupt this uniformity, showing subtle changes in reflectivity or texture. These variations might appear as slightly duller areas, unusual scratches, or patches that reflect light differently from surrounding regions.

Under higher magnification, genuine mint-made features reveal specific characteristics:

- Design elements show crisp transitions from fields to devices
- Metal flow lines radiate consistently from struck areas
- Surface texture maintains uniformity within similar regions
- Strike pressure creates symmetric displacement patterns
- Crystalline structure appears undisturbed under intense light

Altered surfaces tell a different story:

- Tool marks create microscopic parallel lines
- Metal flow patterns show irregular interruptions
- Surface texture changes abruptly between areas
- Pressure patterns lack symmetry or consistency
- Crystalline structure shows evidence of manipulation

The most challenging cases require progressive magnification examination. Start at 10x, noting any suspicious areas. Move to 20x to examine these areas in detail, paying special attention to transitions between fields and devices. At 40x or higher, even skilled alterations reveal their artificial nature through inconsistent metal flow or tool marks.

Digital microscopy has revolutionized this process by allowing a side-by-side comparison of suspicious areas with verified examples. Capture images at identical magnification levels and lighting angles. Genuine mint errors of the same type show remarkable consistency in their microscopic characteristics. Any deviation from these established patterns warrants further investigation.

Remember that different mint errors require different examination techniques. Doubled dies show specific doubling characteristics that mechanical alteration cannot perfectly replicate. Strike errors display distinctive metal flow patterns at their margins. Even seemingly minor variations in surface texture can reveal important authentication clues when you know exactly what to look for.

RED FLAGS FOR COUNTERFEIT ERROR COINS

The seller's hands shook as he placed three 1943 copper cents on my desk at the Baltimore show. "Family heirlooms," he explained, pointing to worn spots that "proved" their age. Something felt wrong, though, the weight of the first piece told the whole story—10% too heavy. Someone had copper-plated steel cents, artificially worn them, then sealed them with lacquer to prevent rust. A genuine 1943 copper cent would make headlines. These wouldn't fool a basic scale.

Weight, diameter, and thickness specifications serve as our first line of defense against counterfeit errors. The U.S. Mint's production standards remained remarkably consistent even when errors occurred. A genuine error coin typically matches standard specifications except where its specific error type demands variation. Understanding these tolerances helps identify suspicious pieces before investing in detailed analysis.

Lincoln cent specifications evolved precise standards: Pre-1982 bronze: 3.11 grams (plus or minus 0.13 grams) Post-1982 copper-plated zinc: 2.5 grams (plus or minus 0.10 grams) Diameter: 19.05mm (variations over 0.1mm warrant investigation) Thickness: 1.55mm (strike errors may alter this measurably)

Even dramatic errors typically maintain some of these specifications. An off-center strike shows proper thickness in its struck portion. Wrong planchet errors match known specifications of their source denomination. When measurements fall outside documented ranges, detailed authentication becomes essential.

Abnormalities in Edge

A collector recently brought me a "broadstruck" Washington quarter with perfectly smooth edges, but his excitement did fade when I explained that U.S. Mint broadstrikes show vestigial reeding—faint impressions where the collar die started to form the reeds before failing. His piece showed evidence of lathe turning, likely from someone grinding off the reeding to simulate a mint error. Edge characteristics often reveal the first clues about a coin's authenticity.

Genuine mint errors display predictable edge patterns. When a coin strikes without its collar, the metal flows outward naturally, creating a distinctive pattern of radial stress lines. These lines appear microscopically consistent, radiating from the center of the strike. Counterfeiters struggle to replicate this pattern because metal responds uniquely to the massive pressure of the minting press.

The Lincoln Cent's plain edge seems simple, but it reveals subtle authentication clues. Genuine broadstruck cents show a slight upward lip where metal escaped the collar. Strike-through errors display consistent indentation patterns. Even partial collar errors, where the collar die slipped during striking, leaving distinctive witness lines that tell us exactly how the metal flowed during production.

Modern counterfeiting techniques often falter at the edge. Machine-lathed edges show circular tool marks under magnification. Chemical reduction leaves peculiar surface textures. Even skilled attempts to replicate mint error edges typically show microscopic inconsistencies in metal flow patterns.

Magnetic Properties

During World War II, the U.S. Mint made millions of steel cents, but today's collectors seek the rare 1943 copper transitional error. For every genuine copper 1943 cent, thousands of counterfeits exist—steel cents ingeniously copper-plated to deceive eager collectors. But counterfeiters, no matter how skillful, have yet to overcome the laws of physics. A forty-dollar magnet has exposed countless fakes, saving untold thousands in potential losses.

Magnetic testing provides quick insight into a coin's composition, though its effectiveness depends on understanding exactly when and how to apply it. The 1943 steel cent stands as the only regular-issue U.S. cent that responds to magnets. This unique characteristic makes magnet testing particularly valuable for authenticating both steel cents and their copper counterparts.

A proper magnetic test requires more finesse than simply sticking a magnet to a coin. Use a rare earth magnet—they're stronger than traditional magnets and provide more definitive results. Hold the magnet slightly above the coin's surface. Genuine 1943 steel cents show strong attraction, while copper-plated counterfeits often display weak or inconsistent magnetic properties due to varying plating thickness.

Beyond 1943 cents, magnetic testing helps authenticate other error types. Wrong planchet errors involving steel cents should show appropriate magnetic properties. Foreign planchet errors might display unexpected magnetic characteristics that help identify their origin. Even some altered date coins reveal themselves through inconsistent magnetic responses where metallic pastes or fillers are used.

Keep in mind that there are testing limits because modern techniques can create sophisticated counterfeits with carefully calibrated magnetic properties. Consider magnetic testing a preliminary screening tool—useful for quick authentication but not definitive proof of genuineness.

Die Characteristics

In the quiet corner of my office, a customer once spread out twelve "doubled dies" he'd inherited. His eyes gleamed with retirement dreams as he pointed out the dramatic doubling on each piece. His confidence wavered when I showed him how every coin displayed identical tooling marks under the microscope—right down to a distinctive scratch pattern in Lincoln's bowtie. No two genuine die varieties, even of the same type, ever match exactly. Each die has its own fingerprint.

The physics of die striking leaves evidence that no counterfeiter has mastered. When a 150-ton press drives metal into a die's recesses, it creates distinctive flow patterns visible under magnification. These patterns tell us exactly how the metal moved during striking. Counterfeiters, working with basic tools and minimal pressure, can't replicate this complex metal movement.

Watch for these revealing signs in modified pieces: The metal flow around doubled elements often runs in the wrong direction. Genuine dies push metal in predictable patterns—all raised areas stay raised, and all recessed areas stay recessed. Counterfeiters frequently violate these basic physical principles, creating impossible metal displacement patterns.

Field areas between design elements expose many fakes. Real dies create consistent texture across the entire surface. Most counterfeiters focus on modifying letters and numbers, neglecting to match the surrounding field texture. This creates jarring transitions that genuine dies never produce.

Date and mint mark alterations require particular scrutiny. The Mint used specific font styles that evolved over time. I've seen countless fakes mix font characteristics from different decades—like combining a 1940s-style "9" with a 1950s-style "5." These impossible combinations immediately mark a piece as artificial.

Some of the most deceptive counterfeits fail because they look too perfect. Genuine dies develop wear patterns, stress marks, and minor defects through use. When a coin shows dramatic doubling but pristine die characteristics, something's wrong. Real dies tell complete stories—counterfeiters often forget crucial chapters.

USING TECHNOLOGY IN AUTHENTICATION

The most valuable error I ever bought sat untouched in its PCGS holder for three days at the 2022 FUN show. Every visual indicator suggested a genuine 1944 steel cent. The price seemed reasonable at $85,000, but something held me back from making an offer. On the final day, I borrowed time on Heritage's XRF analyzer. The reading showed trace elements of nickel—an impossible composition for genuine steel cents. Someone had transformed a common 1944 zinc-coated steel foreign coin into a very convincing, very fake mint error.

Digital microscopy transformed error authentication from art to precision science. Modern USB microscopes capture surface details at up to 1000x magnification, revealing metal flow patterns invisible to traditional loupes. Their real power lies in comparison—capturing images of questioned pieces alongside verified examples exposes subtle differences in strike characteristics, die wear patterns, and surface texture that even experienced eyes might miss.

Spectrometric analysis penetrates beneath surface appearances. Measuring how different wavelengths of light interact with a coin's metal composition, reveals exact percentages of copper, zinc, tin, and trace elements. This precision proves crucial for authenticating transitional errors like 1943 bronze cents or 1944 steel cents, where composition tells the true story. Recent advances in portable spectrometers bring this technology to coin shows and dealers' offices, though interpreting results requires understanding historical mint compositions.

XRF testing adds another dimension by mapping element distribution across a coin's surface. Unlike basic spectrometry, XRF creates detailed composition profiles showing how metals vary at different depths. This capability exposes sophisticated counterfeits that might fool simpler tests. A genuine copper-plated steel cent shows a sharp transition between layers, while artificial copper plating often reveals uneven penetration or contamination from plating chemicals.

The technology continues evolving. Some grading services now employ 3D surface mapping to document error characteristics. Others use ultrasonic thickness gauging to verify planchet specifications. Yet these tools serve expertise rather than replace it—they provide evidence that experienced authenticators interpret within historical and production contexts.

Weight and Measurement Tools

Under a jewelry store's counter in Portland, I found an unusual scale under a jewelry store's counter in Portland—it was a Seederer-Kohlbusch balance precise to 0.001 grams. "Used it for gold," the retiring owner explained. "But it'll tell you more about a coin than most modern digital scales." He was right. That mechanical marvel, calibrated by hand in the 1940s, still outperforms many contemporary instruments when verifying planchet weights.

Precision measurement demands understanding both equipment limits and mint tolerances. Basic digital scales accurate to 0.1 grams suffice for sorting obvious fakes, but serious authentication requires greater precision. Modern analytical balances reaching 0.001-gram accuracy reveal subtle composition variations in planchets. These minute differences often separate genuine errors from altered pieces.

Digital calipers bring similar precision to dimensional analysis. Look for instruments certified accurate to 0.01mm with hardened steel jaws. Measure multiple points around the coin's circumference—genuine planchets show consistent readings while altered pieces often reveal irregular variations. Track these measurements systematically, comparing them against known mint tolerances for the period.

Photography plays a crucial role in documentation, but technique matters more than equipment. Focus stacking software combines multiple images taken at slightly different focal lengths, creating fully detailed records of surface characteristics. Position your lights at 45-degree angles to reveal raised elements. Use consistent camera settings across comparison shots to ensure an accurate representation of color and texture.

A few essential guidelines for error photography:

- Capture baseline shots straight-on under consistent lighting
- Add angled shots to document raised elements and strike characteristics
- Include calibrated scale references in technical documentation
- Maintain identical settings when photographing comparison pieces
- Archive RAW format images for future analysis

These tools work together, each verification method supporting the others. Precise measurements provide objective data, while detailed photography preserves evidence for later study or consultation with other experts.

WHEN TO SEEK PROFESSIONAL AUTHENTICATION

Look, I get that sending a coin for professional authentication feels like admitting defeat. After spending years developing your skills, investing in equipment, and studying every error variety, it's tempting to trust your own judgment completely. I've been there, but twenty years in this business has taught me that even the most experienced collectors and dealers sometimes need another set of eyes—particularly when dealing with five-figure errors that could make or break a collection.

Reputable authentication services do more than just validate our findings. PCGS, NGC, and ANACS employ teams of specialists who examine hundreds of similar pieces each month. Their collective experience often reveals subtle diagnostic points that even seasoned collectors might miss. Their expertise isn't just about spotting fakes—it's about understanding the minute variations that separate common errors from rare ones, and major varieties from minor ones.

Each service brings its own strengths to error authentication. PCGS has built an extensive database of die varieties and error characteristics. NGC's imaging technology helps document strike and planchet errors in unprecedented detail. ANACS, with its long history in variety attribution, excels at identifying previously unlisted die states and progression patterns.

Professional authentication becomes crucial when:

- The error's value exceeds $1,000
- You've discovered a previously unknown variety
- The piece exhibits unusual characteristics
- You're dealing with historically significant errors
- The coin shows mixed indicators of authenticity
- You plan to sell through major auction houses

The investment in professional authentication often pays for itself—either by confirming a valuable find or preventing a costly mistake.

The Authentication Process

Ten years into collecting, I submitted my first coin for certification—a wheat cent with dramatic doubling. I obsessed over every detail of the submission form, triple-wrapped the coin in protective material, and then spent three weeks checking the online tracking daily. The coin came back genuine but listed as machine doubling rather than a doubled die. That experience taught me what most collectors learn the hard way: understanding the authentication process matters as much as the final verdict.

The Process follows a very precise protocol. Initial screening separates obvious non-genuine pieces, saving both time and return shipping costs. Coins passing this stage move to detailed analysis, where experts examine them under various lighting conditions and magnifications. They compare diagnostic points against extensive databases of known varieties and counterfeits.

Modern authentication reveals more than just genuine or counterfeit status. Grading services now provide detailed attribution for many error types. The holder's label might specify the die stage, error category, or variety attribution. Some services even include identification numbers that link to online databases containing detailed diagnostics and comparative images.

Pay attention to specific terminology in the holder:
- "Mechanical Damage" versus "Mint Error"
- "Machine Doubling" versus "Doubled Die"
- "Environmental Damage" versus "Strike Through"
- "Post-Strike Damage" versus "Multiple Strike"

These distinctions affect both collectibility and value. A coin labeled simply "damaged" might actually exhibit rare mint error characteristics that warrant resubmission with better documentation. Conversely, a seemingly dramatic error might receive a more mundane attribution based on diagnostic evidence visible only to trained experts.

Cost Benefit Analysis

Certain things that you might need to take into consideration when deciding on professional authentication aren't obvious at first glance, for instance, a doubled die worth $500 might not seem to justify a $75 certification fee, but that certification could make the difference between a quick sale at full price and months of fielding lowball offers from skeptical buyers. I learned this lesson after spending two years trying to sell an uncertified 1969-S doubled die—potential buyers kept questioning its authenticity despite clear photos and my detailed documentation.

Market dynamics often dictate authentication needs. Major auction houses require certification for significant errors. Online marketplaces increasingly favor slabbed coins for higher-value transactions. Even private collectors, burned by previous purchases, frequently insist on professional authentication for errors above certain price points.

Consider these factors when weighing certification costs:

Time value of money matters. A certified error typically sells faster than its raw counterpart. Quick turnover at a slightly lower profit sometimes beats waiting months for the perfect buyer who trusts their own judgment. Plus, certified coins often command premium prices that more than offset authentication fees.

The certification investment varies by error type. Minor doubled dies might not see enough value increase to justify the expense, however, off-center strikes above 50%, major die breaks, and significant wrong planchet errors almost always benefit from professional validation. The rarer the error, the more crucial certification becomes.

Building relationships with experienced dealers and authenticators provides benefits beyond mere certification. These connections offer:

- Guidance on which pieces warrant professional authentication
- Insights into current market trends and buyer preferences
- Access to comparative examples for initial evaluation
- Feedback on potential purchases before commitment
- Educational opportunities through shared knowledge

Many dealers maintain networks of specialty experts. A trusted dealer might recognize characteristics that suggest consulting a specific authenticator known for expertise with particular error types. These relationships often prevent wasted submission fees on pieces unlikely to certify.

The true value of professional authentication extends beyond the individual coin. Each submission builds your knowledge base. Certification results provide feedback on your attribution skills, helping refine your eye for genuine errors. Even disappointing results contribute to expertise development—teaching subtle diagnostic points you might have missed.

Think of authentication as an investment in both the coin and your collecting journey. The cost of certification pales compared to the price of acquiring sophisticated counterfeits or misattributed varieties. In error collecting, certainty carries its own value.

5

GRADING AND VALUING ERROR COINS

A circulated 1955 doubled die cent recently sold for $15,000 at auction. In the same sale, a technically higher-grade 1958 doubled die brought only $400. Error coin values often defy traditional grading logic—rarity, demand, and historical significance frequently outweigh condition. Understanding this complex relationship between grade and value makes the error-collecting process a special kind of strategic pursuit.

The market for error coins writes its own rules. While most series favor pristine specimens, error collectors often chase pieces that tell compelling stories regardless of grade. Take the 1943 bronze cent that hammered for $250,000 despite heavy circulation wear. Its survival story—escaping detection during the wartime steel transition—matters more than its technical grade. Similarly, a dramatically off-center strike showing a full date commands attention even with considerable wear, while a perfectly centered mint state piece might struggle to find buyers.

This value paradox extends beyond famous rarities. At a Baltimore show, I watched a dealer price two 1972 doubled dies—one graded MS-65 Red at $1,200, the other XF-45 at $2,000. The lower-grade coin showed a dramatically stronger doubling, making it more desirable to specialists who prize dramatic visual impact over technical preservation. Condition matters, but it's just one factor in a complex equation.

Error coin grading demands an understanding of context. A strike-through error's grade might depend more on the clarity of the striking incident than on surface marks. Partial collar errors often show unusual wear patterns that complicate traditional grading standards. Even color designation on copper cents takes on new meaning with errors—original red surfaces might actually detract from the visual appeal of certain strike mistakes.

The relationship between grade and value shifts with error type. Minor doubled dies generally follow traditional grading premiums since many examples exist across grade ranges, then major rarities like the 1969-S doubled die break this pattern—even heavily circulated pieces command five-figure prices. Off-center strikes above 50% tend to hold value well regardless of grade, while lesser off-centers need high grades to generate significant premiums.

This complexity demands a different approach to collecting strategy, an understanding of not just grading standards, but how different error categories interact with condition, rarity, and market demand. The following pages will break down these relationships, providing frameworks for evaluating both technical grade and market value across major error types.

UNDERSTANDING GRADING CODES FOR E RROR COINS

You might have noticed that I've been using codes like MS-65 or AU-58 throughout this book. These grades represent standardized measures of condition and quality, developed over decades of professional numismatic evaluation. When a 1955 doubled die cent moves from MS-66 to MS-67, its value can increase by $25,000 or more. That single grade point illustrates why understanding these codes proves crucial for serious error collecting.

The grading scale originated with early copper large cents but evolved to encompass every coin type, including errors. Today, these grades provide precise communication between collectors, dealers, and auction houses. When I describe an MS-64 Red strike-through error, another dealer in San Francisco knows exactly what surface quality to expect, even without photos.

Here is the breakdown of the codes that define coin grades. MS-70 represents absolute perfection, though, in error coins, this grade appears rarely—even more rarely than in regular issues. A true MS-70 error must display flawless surfaces while exhibiting perfect execution of its error characteristics.

The Mint State (MS) grades work down from there:

- MS-69: Virtual perfection. Two or three microscopic flaws might exist

- MS-68: Exceptional quality with minimal imperfections

- MS-67: Strong eye appeal with minor contact marks visible under magnification

- MS-66: Above average with scattered small marks or slight imperfections

- MS-65: Choice quality showing minor scattered marks

- MS-64: Above average with noticeable but not detracting marks

- MS-63: Average mint state with numerous small marks or few larger ones

- MS-61 to MS-62: Below average mint state showing heavy bag marks

About Uncirculated (AU) grades indicate minimal wear:
- AU-58: Traces of wear on highest points, nearly full mint luster

- AU-55: Light wear on elevated features, considerable mint luster

- AU-53: Clear wear but more than half of mint luster remains

- AU-50: Moderate wear with some mint luster in protected areas

Extremely Fine (XF) grades show defined wear patterns:
- XF-45: Light even wear on all high points

- XF-40: Moderate wear with clear detail remaining

Very Fine (VF) grades display more extensive wear:
- VF-35: Clear design detail despite obvious wear

- VF-20: All major features clear but well worn

For Lincoln cent errors specifically, grading services might add color designations:
- RD (Red): Original mint color, at least 95% intact

- RB (Red-Brown): Mixture of original red and brown toning

- BN (Brown): Complete color change from original mint red

Special modifiers for error coins include:
- FB: Full Bands (for Mercury dimes)

- FBL: Full Bell Lines (for Franklin halves)

- FS: Full Steps (for Jefferson nickels)

These designations carry special significance when they appear on error pieces, often commanding significant premiums.

UNDERSTANDING THE ERROR GRADING SCALE

Professional graders often say error grading requires forgetting half of what you know about normal coin grading while doubling down on the other half. I learned this the hard way at the 2018 FUN show when my carefully curated collection of mint errors went for certification. My MS-65 candidate—a dramatic strike-through showing crystal-clear fabric impressions—came back MS-67, meanwhile, my seemingly pristine off-center piece, with virtually no marks, earned just MS-63 due to strike weakness in the error area. That day transformed my understanding of how the Sheldon scale adapts to error coins.

Traditional grading emphasizes surface preservation, strike quality, and eye appeal. Error grading reshuffles these priorities. A mint state off-center strike must show strong design detail where struck, but minor bag marks in the blank portion barely impact the grade. Die breaks earn higher grades for sharp, clear separation along the break line, even if other areas show contact marks. Even luster patterns, crucial for regular issues, take a back seat to error feature clarity on many varieties.

The complexity deepens when evaluating circulated errors; wear patterns that would doom a normal coin might represent expected characteristics on certain error types. Partial collar errors often show uneven wear. Multiple strikes create complex patterns that demand entirely different evaluation criteria. Some errors, like certain die breaks, actually become more distinct with light circulation.

The 70-point scale itself remains, but its application shifts dramatically across error categories. An MS-70 doubled die must show perfect surfaces and strong separation in the doubled elements. Yet an MS-70 strike-through might display what appears to be damage—if that "damage" clearly shows the struck-through material's characteristics. These nuances separate experienced error collectors from traditional grading experts.

Modern certification has brought more consistency to error grading, but understanding these specialized standards remains crucial for collectors and dealers alike. The grade assigned often reflects not just the condition, but how well the coin displays its particular error characteristics.

Specific Grading Considerations

Off-center strikes demand unique evaluation methods. At the 2022 Long Beach Expo, a dealer showed me two 50% off-center Lincoln cents. Both displayed similar wear, yet one graded AU-58 while the other settled at AU-50. The difference? Strike quality in the design portion. Even with identical preservation, the higher-grade piece showed sharper design detail where struck, particularly in Lincoln's hair and the wheat stalks. This illustrates how strike characteristics often outweigh traditional wear patterns when grading off-center pieces.

Doubled dies present their own complexity. The strength of doubling directly influences grade, sometimes more than surface quality. A 1972 doubled die cent might grade MS-65 despite noticeable contact marks if it displays exceptional separation in the doubled elements. Conversely, a technically pristine piece showing weak doubling might struggle to exceed MS-63. The grading services evaluate both traditional criteria and the clarity of the doubled features.

Net grading becomes crucial when examining coins with multiple attributes. Consider a recent submission I handled: an MS-64 1955 doubled die showed evidence of cleaning but displayed exceptional doubling strength. The grading service assigned a net grade of AU-58, acknowledging both the technical grade and the surface alteration. This balance between condition and enhancement affects market value significantly.

Strike-through errors require evaluating seemingly contradictory elements. Surface deformation that would normally detract from grade might represent the error's most valuable characteristic. A 1964 cent struck through fabric recently graded MS-66 despite what appeared to be significant surface damage—the "damage" actually preserved a perfect impression of the fabric weave.

- Specific grade indicators vary by error type:
- **For partial collar errors:** Sharpness of the step between normal and stretched rim
- **For die breaks:** Clarity of the break's edges and completeness of the cud
- **For wrong planchets:** Surface preservation and strike quality on visible design elements
- **For rotated dies:** Completeness of design detail on both sides despite rotation

Modern grading services maintain detailed criteria for each error category. They examine:

- Strike completeness where design exists
- Quality of error characteristics
- Surface preservation in critical areas
- Overall eye appeal within error context

VALUABLE LINCOLN PENNY ERROR COIN HANDBOOK

- Metal flow patterns typical for the error type

These standards evolve with market preferences, some might have been graded MS-63 ten years ago and could qualify for MS-64 or MS-65 today, as graders develop a better understanding of how specific errors should appear.

FACTORS AFFECTING THE VALUE OF ERROR COINS

The 1922 "No D" cent that landed on my desk last month taught me something vital about error coin values. Every technical aspect suggested a $15,000 retail price, and it still sold within hours at $22,500. That's because the strike characteristics displayed the clearest example of die deterioration I'd seen in twenty years of specializing in this variety. This transaction reinforced what experienced dealers already know: while certain factors like rarity and grade provide baseline values, exceptional pieces create their own markets.

Rarity

Pure population numbers tell only part of the story. Consider the 1955 doubled die cent. Estimates suggest 24,000 were minted, yet fewer than 3,500 survive in collectible condition. Among these, perhaps 100 exist in Mint State grades. True rarity encompasses both original mintage and survival rates. The 1943 bronze cent demonstrates this principle perfectly—while roughly twenty pieces were struck, only twelve survive today, creating one of the most valuable Lincoln cent errors.

Historical Significance

Certain errors transcend mere rarity through their connection to significant mint events. The 1944 steel cent represents more than just a wrong planchet error—it documents the transition from wartime necessity back to standard composition. Similarly, the 1969-S doubled die cent reveals a crucial moment in mint quality control practices. These historical connections add substantial premium value beyond condition or rarity considerations.

Condition and Grade

Error coins challenge traditional grading relationships. While higher grades typically command better prices, the value curve varies dramatically by error type. Major doubled dies follow predictable grade-to-value progression because enough examples exist across grade ranges to establish clear pricing patterns, however, rare wrong planchet errors or dramatic strike errors might show minimal value difference between XF and AU grades because their defining characteristics matter more than absolute preservation.

Visual Appeal

The visual impact of an error often drives its market value beyond standard pricing guidelines. A 50% off-center strike showing a complete date carries significantly more value than a 45% off-center piece, though the technical difference is minimal. Strike-through errors that clearly show the causing object's detail command premiums over similar pieces with less distinct impressions. Even within the same variety, such as the 1972 doubled die cent, examples showing stronger doubling routinely sell for 50% more than weakly doubled pieces in the same grade.

Market Trends and Demand

Market dynamics for error coins operate independently from regular issue trends. While traditional series might see broad market swings, error collecting tends toward specialty niches with their own supply-demand patterns. The emergence of registry set collecting has dramatically increased demand for highest-grade examples of popular varieties. Social media has created instant markets for newly discovered error types, sometimes establishing significant values before traditional price guides can react.

PRICE GUIDES AND RESOURCES FOR VALUATION

Twenty years ago, determining an error coin's value meant waiting months for the latest price guide to arrive by mail. Now, my phone buzzes with Heritage auction results seconds after the hammer falls. This real-time market data has transformed how we price errors, yet understanding which resources to trust—and how to interpret their information—matters more than ever.

Print Resources

The CPG Guide has evolved beyond simple price listings for error coins. Their quarterly updates include detailed market analysis of major varieties and emerging trends. The guide particularly excels at tracking doubled die values across all grades. While prices may lag behind fast-moving markets, their historical data helps identify long-term value patterns for specific error types.

The Cherry Picker's Guide stands alone in its approach to error coin values. Rather than just listing prices, it provides relative rarity ratings that help dealers and collectors gauge potential value, especially for newly discovered varieties. Its attribution photos and diagnostics prove invaluable when authenticating valuable errors before purchase.

Online Auction Archives

Heritage Auctions' database has revolutionized error coin valuation. Their archived prices, dating back over twenty years, show how specific error types perform across different market conditions. The high-resolution photos accompanying each lot help establish condition benchmarks for similar pieces. Their "Make an Offer" section reveals what collectors actually pay, not just asking prices.

Stack's Bowers maintains detailed records of error coin transactions, including many pieces that never appeared in traditional price guides. Their archive proves particularly valuable for tracking values of major rarities like the 1943 bronze cent or 1969-S doubled die. Their detailed lot descriptions often include attribution information that helps establish value parameters for similar errors.

Market Analysis Websites

PCGS CoinFacts combines population data with recent sales information, that offers you insight into how availability affects value. Their price history graphs reveal patterns that help predict future market movements for major error types. The site's condition census proves particularly valuable when evaluating high-grade pieces.

NGC's Price Guide approaches error values differently, breaking down prices by both grade and variety attribution. Their certified population reports help determine relative rarity within specific error categories. The site excels at tracking values for modern error types that traditional guides might overlook.

Independent Market Resources

Error-Variety.com maintains current market data for doubled dies and RPMs, often catching value trends before they appear in mainstream guides. Their forum discussions frequently reveal regional market variations and collector preferences that affect values.

CONECA's Errorscope publication provides specialized market analysis for new discoveries and emerging error types. Their attribution files help establish baseline values for previously unknown varieties, particularly valuable in today's rapid-response market environment.

HOW TO INTERPRET AND USE PRICE GUIDES EFFECTIVELY

A prominent dealer once listed a 1972 doubled die cent for $4,800, citing three recent auction sales, though he failed to notice a crucial detail—those examples showed dramatically stronger doubling than his piece. Price guides and auction records provide essential data, but extracting meaningful value information requires understanding the subtle factors that influence individual coin values.

Published Prices vs. Real Market

Listed values serve as starting points rather than absolute figures. Recent auction sales of a 1955 doubled die in MS-65 ranged from $25,000 to $42,000. The difference? Strike quality and eye appeal. The highest price came from an example with exceptional doubling clarity and original mint red color. The lowest represented a technically sound but visually unremarkable piece.

Time-Based Analysis

Track sales patterns across months or years, not just recent transactions. When I researched values for the 1969-S doubled die, sales from 2018 through 2023 revealed consistent price increases in high grades but stability in circulated examples. This pattern helped identify which grades offered the best value for long-term holding.

Population Impact

Compare prices against certified populations. The 1944 D/S cent might show similar prices in VF-20 and VF-30, despite the higher grade. Why? The population data reveals nearly equal numbers in both grades, suggesting neither commands a significant premium over the other.

Condition Specifics

Price guides often list generic grades like "MS-65" without noting crucial details. For copper cents, the difference between Red, Red-Brown, and Brown dramatically affects value. A 1958 doubled die in MS-65 Red might bring triple the price of the same coin in MS-65 Brown.

Market Context

Consider the market segment when evaluating prices. Registry set collectors often pay significant premiums for the highest-grade examples of popular varieties. Meanwhile, casual collectors typically focus on mid-grade pieces, creating different price dynamics across grade ranges.

Authentication Status

Factor in certification costs and value differences between raw and certified coins. Some error types command a minimal premium when certified, while others practically require certification for sale. Understanding these market preferences helps evaluate whether certification will enhance resale value.

While price guides do provide frameworks for valuation, meaningful price interpretation requires synthesizing multiple data points with market knowledge. Successful dealers and collectors know this because they develop systematic approaches to price analysis, considering all relevant factors before making purchase or sale decisions.

GETTING COINS PROFESSIONALLY GRADED

Certain instances require that you pursue professional certification, even when your attribution skills and market knowledge feel solid. This reality hit home at last year's Long Beach Expo. A dealer displayed two 1969-S doubled dies with nearly identical characteristics. The certified piece commanded $28,000 and sold within hours. Its uncertified twin, despite matching visual appeal and seemingly equal quality, struggled to attract interest at $18,000. This $10,000 gap represents exactly how professional certification has become integral to serious error coin trading.

PROFESSIONAL CERTIFICATION SERVICES (PCGS)

PCGS built its reputation through consistent grading standards and holder security. Their expertise particularly shines with doubled dies and repunched mint marks. The service maintains a detailed variety of attributions, often identifying specific die stages that affect value. Their holders include crucial details about error characteristics that help justify premium values.

Numismatic Guaranty Corporation (NGC)

NGC approaches error certification with a distinct methodology. Their detailed descriptions often capture subtle characteristics that other services might overlook. They excel at attributing modern errors and providing thorough documentation of strike characteristics. Their photography department particularly excels at capturing evidence of error features.

American Numismatic Association Certification Service (ANACS)

ANACS leverages its position as the oldest grading service through deep expertise in variety attribution. They often recognize previously unlisted varieties, particularly in doubled dies and repunched mint marks. Their variety attribution numbers help track different die stages, crucial for establishing relative rarity.

Deciding When to Grade

- Major value thresholds often determine grading decisions:
- Doubled dies above VF-20 typically benefit from certification
- Off-center strikes above 50% command premium prices when certified
- Wrong planchet errors almost always justify grading costs
- Die breaks showing full cuds need certification for optimal value
- Previously undocumented varieties require certification to establish credibility

Service Selection Factors

Each service brings unique strengths:
- PCGS: Highest market premiums for major varieties
- NGC: Superior holder design for displaying error characteristics
- ANACS: Most detailed variety attribution

Consider these factors alongside current market preferences when selecting services.

Modern developments in holder technology have enhanced error coin display and protection. UV-resistant holders better preserve the original color on copper cents. Clear holders showcase error characteristics from multiple angles. These technological advances increasingly influence service selection for specific error types.

THE SUBMISSION PROCESS

The submission process requires methodical attention to detail, starting with meticulous careful coin preparation. Clean cotton gloves protect surfaces from fingerprints. Every coin needs secure individual packaging—I prefer high-quality mylar flips secured with removable tape. Never clean coins before submission; grading services interpret any attempt at improvement as surface alteration.

Submission Forms and Documentation Each service maintains specific requirements:

PCGS requires:
- Accurate variety attribution numbers when known
- Detailed error descriptions for unlisted varieties
- Current membership number
- Declaration of any known surface problems
- Selection of service level affecting turnaround time Minimum submissions vary by service level—five coins for regular submissions, one coin for expensive varieties.

NGC emphasizes:
- Clear identification of error type
- Any recognized variety numbers
- Specific requests for recognized designations
- Selection of service tier They particularly value detailed descriptions of newly discovered varieties.

Understanding Service Levels

Standard submission typically takes 20-30 days Express service: 10 business days Walk-through service: 24 hours Costs increase significantly with faster service levels. Express might cost triple the standard rate, while walk-through commands premium pricing but proves valuable for time-sensitive authentications.

Holder Information Interpretation Modern holders contain crucial details about your coin:

Variety attribution numbers link to online databases
- Specific error descriptions define characteristic types
- Grade reflects both technical quality and error features
- Special designations note exceptional characteristics

- Certification number enables online verification
- Green label versus regular label indicates specific varieties

Serial numbers on holders provide production date information. Early PCGS holders used different label formats—understanding these changes helps authenticate older certifications. NGC's recent holder modifications improved error visibility while maintaining security features.

Common Submission Mistakes

- Incorrect variety attribution
- Wrong service level selection
- Incomplete documentation
- Poor packaging leading to shipping damage
- Failure to declare known problems

These errors can delay processing or result in coins being returned ungraded. Multiple submission attempts due to poor preparation often exceed the cost of proper initial submission.

The grading services regularly update their submission requirements. Current forms, shipping instructions, and pricing information require verification before each submission. Membership levels might affect both costs and service options—annual membership fees often pay for themselves through reduced submission rates.

6

BUILDING YOUR LINCOLN PENNY ERROR COLLECTION

One of the most satisfying feelings is watching certainty replace confusion. During my first year examining Lincoln cents, I pulled aside hundreds of "errors" that weren't errors at all. Machine doubling fooled me constantly. Strike variations that meant nothing excited me endlessly. That changed when a dealer at the Memphis show spent an hour showing me the subtle indicators I'd missed on every coin. He taught me to look past the obvious and spot the authentic signs of genuine errors.

Now, after decades of handling these pieces, those early lessons prove invaluable. When I spread potential errors across my desk, true varieties announce themselves through distinct characteristics. Each legitimate doubled die shows specific patterns. Authentic strike errors display telling signs. Yet reaching this point required more than just time—it demanded deliberate decisions about which pieces deserved space in my collection.

The current market presents unique opportunities and challenges. Digital imaging reveals microscopic details. Certification services document new varieties weekly. Yet this abundance of information and access also means more ways to waste time and resources chasing the wrong pieces. Success requires a clear purpose, defined goals, and tested strategies. This chapter reveals the approaches that separate significant collections from random accumulations.

DEVELOPING A COLLECTING STRATEGY

Like real wealth is built over decades through careful investment strategies, significant error collections develop through deliberate choices and focused acquisition plans. At a recent Baltimore show, I watched a new collector buy three minor doubled dies for the price of one major variety. He chose quantity over quality, a common early mistake that delays building a truly noteworthy collection.

The most successful error collections I've handled share clear themes. Some focus exclusively on doubled dies from the 1950s, documenting the era's distinctive hub and die characteristics. Others concentrate on dramatic off-centers above 50%, showing how strike alignment variations affect design elements. A few ambitious collectors pursue every known die stage of the 1972 doubled die, revealing how dies deteriorated during production.

Your collecting strategy should align with both market reality and personal interests. Major doubled dies command strong prices but appear infrequently. Strike errors surface more often but require deeper knowledge to authenticate properly. Some collectors focus on specific dates, like 1944 when changing composition created numerous possibilities for wrong planchet errors. Others pursue error types across multiple decades to show how production methods evolved.

Consider these factors when defining your focus:
- Available budget and purchase frequency
- Local dealer inventory and access to major shows
- Storage and display requirements
- Authentication resources in your area
- Long-term market trends for specific error types
- Personal knowledge of certain varieties

A focused strategy transforms random purchases into curated acquisitions. Each new piece should advance your collecting goals while fitting within established parameters. This approach not only builds stronger collections but often reveals overlooked opportunities in familiar error categories.

Balancing Rarity, Condition, and Budget

At every major show, collectors face the same decision—buy one exceptional piece or several lesser examples. Last month in Chicago, a collector chose three VF-20 doubled dies over a single MS-63 example. "More coins mean more collection," he insisted. Six months later, he realized his mistake. Those three lower-grade pieces proved difficult to sell, while similar MS-63 pieces had risen 20% in value.

Budget constraints force hard choices. A single 1955 doubled die in AU-50 might cost as much as twenty minor varieties in high grade. Yet experience shows that major rarities in problem-free circulated grades often appreciate more than common varieties in mint state. Consider the 1969-S doubled die—even well-worn examples command five figures because population matters more than preservation.

Strategic collecting requires understanding value dynamics: High-grade common errors often lag behind Mid-grade major varieties show consistent strength Key dates in any grade maintain collector demand strike characteristics often outweigh technical grade Eye appeal can trump numerical grade assignments.

Building an effective want list means more than recording dates and varieties. Track recent sales of similar pieces. Note certification service population changes. Document condition rarity within specific varieties. This data helps identify opportunities when they appear.

Your want list should include:

- Target grades for each variety
- Price points that represent value
- Known population figures
- Recent auction results
- Specific diagnostic points to verify
- Notable examples and their characteristics

Strategies for Upgrading Your Collection Over Time

Successful collectors maintain flexible priorities. When exceptional pieces appear, they adjust acquisition plans, they recognize that opportunities to acquire significant errors often arise unexpectedly, so having clear parameters helps make quick decisions when important pieces surface.

Smart dealers rarely keep their first example of any major error variety; that MS-63 1972 doubled die you bought last year? It serves as leverage when an MS-65 appears. The VF-35 off-center strike that started your collection? Consider it a placeholder until a superior example surfaces. Strategic upgrading builds stronger collections while often funding future purchases.

Market timing influences upgrading decisions. In 2019, a collector sold his MS-64 Red Brown 1955 doubled die for $12,000. Instead of banking the profit, he added $8,000 and secured an MS-65 Red example. Today, that MS-65 Red commands $45,000, while the MS-64 Red Brown trades near $15,000. His strategic upgrade tripled his potential return.

Upgrading requires discipline and documentation:

- Track condition census changes
- Monitor auction prices across grades
- Document surface quality of current pieces
- Maintain detailed photographs for comparisons
- Network with dealers specializing in upgrades
- Build relationships with collectors holding superior pieces

Consider strike quality when upgrading doubled dies. An MS-63 showing strong doubling often outperforms an MS-65 with weak doubling. For off-center strikes, completeness of design sometimes matters more than technical grade. Wrong planchet errors derive value more from planchat composition clarity than surface marks.

Some collectors maintain two-tier collections. They acquire affordable examples to study varieties while simultaneously building a premium set. This approach provides hands-on learning opportunities without compromising long-term collection quality. When superior pieces appear, they already understand the variety's characteristics.

The strongest collections emerge from systematic upgrading. Each improvement should represent significant advancement, not merely incremental changes. The difference between MS-64 and MS-65 must justify the additional investment. Sometimes waiting for the right piece proves more profitable than making marginal improvements.

Where To Find Errors

Most error collectors start with bank boxes, yet few understand how dramatically the circulation search game has changed. In 1998, I found a 1995 doubled die in my first box of searched cents. Today, that same variety might take 400 boxes to locate. Bank rolls now undergo multiple machine sorts and collector searches before reaching your hands. Yet circulation searching still yields results—if you approach it systematically.

Modern searching demands efficiency. Start by creating a workspace with proper lighting and a magnifier stand. Examine rolls from banks that receive commercial deposits rather than rolled customer coins. These sources typically contain older dates and see fewer collector searches. Business deposits, particularly from rural areas, sometimes yield coins that bypassed years of circulation.

Develop a routine that balances speed with accuracy:

- Box placement matters—position them for smooth roll handling
- Sort by decade first to isolate promising date ranges
- Check reverse sides for dramatic errors visible at arm's length
- Use angle lighting to spot raised areas indicating doubling
- Remove obvious damaged pieces quickly
- Focus extended examination on promising specimens

Certain dates deserve extra scrutiny:

- 1969-1972 (multiple known doubled dies)
- 1983-1984 (transition years with composition errors)
- 1992-1995 (several significant doubled dies)
- 1998-2000 (wide AM varieties)
- Recent dates showing unusual strike characteristics

Commercial coin-counting machines have changed circulation patterns. These machines often trap significant errors due to weight or size variations. Some collectors develop relationships with bank branches that service these machines, arranging to examine rejected coins. These relationships occasionally yield major finds that automatic sorters missed.

Record keeping transforms random searching into meaningful research:

- Track which bank branches yield better results
- Document search volumes and find rates
- Note patterns in date distributions
- Monitor changes in coin quality by source
- Compare results across different areas

While major varieties rarely surface in circulation today, many collectible errors still emerge from careful searching. Modern strike errors, minor doubled dies, and die breaks appear regularly. Understanding which pieces warrant closer examination helps maximize searching efficiency.

Coin Roll Hunting

Bank relationships determine access to promising rolls. The difference between regular consumer-wrapped rolls and commercial deposits proves significant. Commercial deposits, particularly from small businesses like laundromats and vending operators, often contain coins that escaped years of collector searching. Strategic relationships with multiple banks increase your chances—when one branch runs low, others can fill the gap.

Create an efficient roll processing system:

- Set up a dedicated sorting area
- Use a compartmentalized tray for different finds
- Keep detailed records of which banks yield results
- Track time invested versus finds made
- Store examined coins separately to avoid reprocessing

Local Coin Shops and Dealers

Independent coin shops often overlook error varieties while processing bulk purchases. One dealer I know sets aside every doubled die candidate, regardless of attribution certainty. He sells these pieces at minimal markup to regular customers who help identify significant varieties. This arrangement benefits both parties—the dealer maintains steady business while collectors access fresh material.

Building productive dealer relationships requires:

- Regular visits even when not buying
- Sharing knowledge about new varieties
- Offering fair prices on both purchases and sales
- Providing quick decisions on offered material
- Maintaining professional communication

Online Marketplaces

eBay's search algorithms favor specific listing patterns. Serious error collectors create saved searches using multiple keyword combinations. "Double die" finds different listings than "doubled die." Some sellers misspell variety names, creating opportunities for knowledgeable buyers. Many significant errors sell for minimal prices due to poor listings or inadequate photographs.

Successful online buying strategies:
- Monitor newly listed items daily
- Save searches for specific varieties
- Study seller feedback patterns
- Request additional photos when needed
- Verify return policies before bidding
- Track sold prices to identify market trends

Coin Shows and Conventions

Major shows require strategic planning. Create a show schedule identifying key dealers known for error inventory. First-day attendance often yields better selection but higher prices. Last-day shopping might reveal bargains as dealers reduce inventory for travel. Mid-size regional shows frequently offer better values than national events.

Maximize show effectiveness by:
- Arriving early on opening day
- Bringing reference materials
- Carrying proper lighting and magnification
- Networking with specialty dealers
- Maintaining want lists with price targets

Social Media and Online Communities

Error collecting groups on Facebook and specialized forums provide market intelligence and trading opportunities. Members often share new discoveries, allowing early identification of emerging varieties. Some groups maintain databases of known errors, helping authenticate potential purchases.

Effective online networking involves:
- Regular contribution to discussions
- Sharing knowledge when appropriate

- Building reputation through accurate attribution
- Maintaining professional relationships
- Following established trading protocols

Each source requires different approaches and yields different opportunities. Success comes from developing systematic methods for monitoring and evaluating potential purchases across all channels.

COIN ROLL HUNTING TECHNIQUES

Coin roll hunting involves more finesse than what you might assume. Showing up at random banks asking for multiple boxes of pennies creates resistance. Instead, establish relationships through regular business. Open accounts, maintain reasonable balances, and demonstrate professionalism. Some of my best sources came from branch managers who recognized my serious approach to the hobby.

Most banks limit penny box orders without prior arrangements. Large orders require advance notice—typically 48 hours for multiple boxes. Some branches partner with commercial coin suppliers who charge fees for large orders. Understanding these policies before making requests saves time and maintains goodwill.

Successful roll hunting relies on strategic bank selection:

- Branches in older neighborhoods often yield vintage coins
- Commercial deposit-heavy locations provide fresh material
- Small-town banks sometimes store older rolls longer

- Branches near colleges frequently receive parent-cleaned collections
- Rural locations might bypass typical sorting processes

Professional conduct matters:

- Order reasonable quantities
- Schedule pickup times and stick to them
- Return searched rolls wrapped properly
- Maintain separate accounts for coin transactions
- Process returns at less busy times
- Keep friendly but professional relationships with staff

Remember that banks provide a service, not a coin-hunting resource. Your collecting activities should never disrupt normal operations or inconvenience other customers. This approach ensures continued access to fresh rolls while maintaining positive relationships with bank staff.

Proper Etiquette

When Returning Coins Bank operations depend on properly prepared returns. Machine-wrapped rolls meet commercial standards, while hand-wrapped rolls often jam counting machines. Invest in a quality coin tubing machine—the $200 cost pays for itself through maintained bank relationships. Never return loose coins or poorly wrapped rolls; this practice marks you as an amateur and might terminate your hunting privileges.

Branch managers notice presentations. Clean, organized boxes show respect for their time. Sort returns by denomination if mixing other coins from searching. Schedule returns during slower periods—never during lunch rushes or closing time. Some branches prefer specific days for large returns; learn these preferences and adapt accordingly.

Quality control matters:

- Remove damaged or bent coins
- Eliminate foreign pieces
- Sort out silver coins if found
- Remove severely corroded pieces
- Check for stuck rolls before returning
- Ensure accurate coin counts

Record-Keeping Systems

Detailed records are necessary, most successful roll hunters maintain comprehensive databases that reveal patterns over time. Start with basic box information—source, date, and acquisition details. Note whether rolls appear machine-wrapped or customer-wrapped, as this often indicates searching history. Track the branch manager or teller who provided the order, building a network of reliable sources.

Time investment analysis proves crucial for long-term success. Record start and finish times for each searching session. Monitor how many rolls you process per hour and how this rate varies based on the date ranges encountered. Some hunters find they search pre-1982 copper cents slower than modern zinc cents. This data helps optimize future searching efficiency.

Variety documentation requires particular attention to detail. When you find an error or variety, record its full attribution, specific die characteristics, and condition details. Photograph significant pieces immediately, capturing diagnostic points under consistent lighting. Note the position within the roll—some hunters find patterns in how errors cluster in commercial rolls.

Date distribution tracking reveals valuable patterns. Record percentage breakdowns by decade and unusual concentrations of specific dates. Note mint mark patterns and composition changes. Some branches consistently yield older dates, while others provide primarily recent mintages. This information helps target future box orders more effectively.

Branch performance metrics guide strategic decisions. Calculate find rates per box from each source. Track the quality of rolls received and the percentage of machine-wrapped versus customer-wrapped rolls. Note how these patterns shift seasonally—some branches yield better results during specific months.

Your standardized logging system should include regular photography of significant finds, specific measurements of varieties, and detailed die stage documentation. Track market values of discoveries and maintain notes about authentication potential. This documentation proves invaluable when deciding whether to submit pieces for certification.

Digital organization ensures long-term access to your data. Use cloud storage for backup and maintain a searchable format that allows quick reference. Regular analysis of this information reveals patterns in branch productivity, best acquisition times, and most efficient search methods. These insights transform random searching into systematic collection building.

Realistic Expectations

Modern roll hunting yields different results than decades past. In 1995, searching 10 boxes might reveal several collectible errors. Today, that same effort might produce one or two minor varieties. Commercial sorting machines remove many errors before rolls reach banks. Understanding current success rates helps set reasonable goals.

Average findings per $500 box:

- Minor doubled dies: 0-1 per 5 boxes
- Strike errors: 1-2 per box
- Die breaks: 2-3 per box
- Significant varieties: 1 per 20-30 boxes
- Major errors: 1 per 100+ boxes

Success requires volume and persistence. Serious hunters process multiple boxes weekly. They develop efficient systems for quick variety identification while maintaining accuracy. Most importantly, they understand that significant finds come from consistent effort rather than lucky breaks.

The modern roll hunting environment demands adaptation. Some hunters coordinate with multiple branches to ensure a steady supply. Others develop relationships with commercial coin processors. Success comes from treating roll hunting as a systematic process rather than a casual hobby.

ATTENDING COIN SHOWS AND AUCTIONS

Navigating large shows requires discipline. That pristine doubled die might look tempting, but does it fit your collection goals? Successful collectors check every piece against their want list and budget. They examine coins methodically, using consistent lighting and magnification. When they find significant pieces, they document diagnostics before negotiating.

Professional conduct opens doors. Dealers remember collectors who handle coins carefully and ask informed questions. They notice who takes time to learn about varieties before making offers. Simple courtesies—like not interrupting other customers' transactions or asking permission before using your own loupe—build relationships that lead to first looks at new inventory.

Auction participation demands different skills. Unlike show floors where you can examine pieces personally, auctions require confident bidding based on photos and descriptions. Successful bidders know exact market values and set firm limits. They factor in buyer's premiums, shipping costs, and potential certification fees before raising their hands.

Major auctions move quickly. That 1955 doubled die you've been watching might take thirty seconds to sell. Preparation means knowing your maximum bid, understanding the auctioneer's increment patterns, and recognizing when to hold back. Some of the best deals come from knowing when not to bid.

BUILDING RELATIONSHIPS WITH DEALERS AND COLLECTORS

Good things aren't built in isolation, they're built by forming solid connections. My most significant error acquisition came through a dealer who remembered my interest in doubled dies. He called me first when an unlisted variety crossed his desk. That opportunity arose not from luck, but from years of consistent interaction and honest dealing.

Trust in numismatics develops through patterns of behavior. Dealers notice who studies their material carefully, makes fair offers, and follows through on commitments. They remember collectors who share knowledge about varieties rather than simply trying to exploit dealer oversight. These interactions create relationships that transcend simple buying and selling.

Local coin clubs provide unique opportunities for growth. During monthly meetings, experienced collectors often share diagnostics for detecting specific varieties. Club auctions sometimes yield overlooked errors, while show-and-tell sessions reveal new discoveries. More importantly, regular attendance demonstrates a commitment to the hobby, opening doors to private collections and dealer inventories.

Online forums extend your network globally but require careful navigation. Contribute meaningful content before seeking advice. Document your discoveries with quality photos and detailed descriptions. When questions arise about attribution or authenticity, acknowledge uncertainty rather than making definitive claims. Your digital reputation follows you to physical coin shows.

Ethical dealing forms the foundation of lasting relationships. When you spot an underpriced rarity in a dealer's case, pointing it out might cost a profit opportunity but gains long-term trust. If you discover an attribution mistake that works in your favor, addressing it openly earns respect. The numismatic community remembers both integrity and its absence.

Trading between collectors demands clear communication. Document condition issues thoroughly. Provide detailed photos before shipping. State terms explicitly, especially regarding return privileges. Some of the strongest collecting relationships start through trades, but only when both parties prioritize transparency over short-term advantage.

7

PRESERVING AND DISPLAYING YOUR COLLECTION

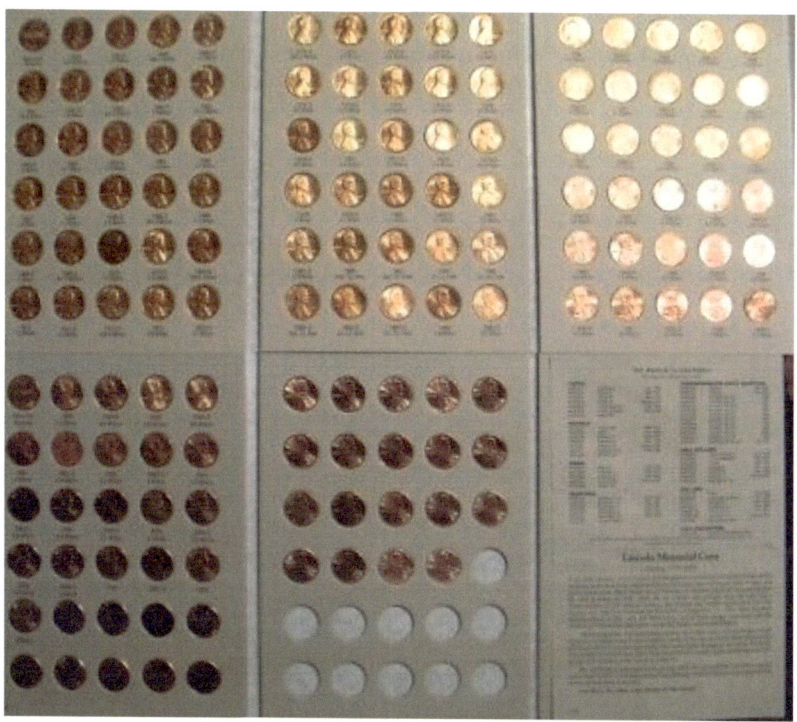

Copper cents tell unforgiving stories about their storage history. That seemingly innocent cardboard album from 1960 might have protected against physical damage, but its sulfur content gradually turned pristine red surfaces to mottled brown. Modern preservation methods help avoid such costly lessons, protecting both condition and value.

The science of numismatic preservation has evolved dramatically. We now understand how seemingly minor factors—humidity levels, air pollutants, plastic compositions—affect coin surfaces over time. Materials once considered state-of-the-art have proven destructive. Those green folder albums from the 1950s, though beautifully designed, contained chemicals that actively damaged coins. The popular PVC flips of the 1970s left sticky residues that still plague coins today.

Every collection tells these preservation stories through its surfaces. A 1955 doubled die might grade MS-65, but improper storage can trigger subtle changes that reduce eye appeal without technically lowering the grade. Even certified coins require proper environmental conditions—holders protect against physical contact but can't prevent all forms of environmental damage.

Over the next few pages, we'll examine storage options, environmental controls, and display techniques specifically suited to error coins, so that you can prevent costly mistakes while maintaining your collection's long-term potential.

PROPER HANDLING TECHNIQUES

I overheard someone once say that your coins should be handled in the same way that you'd handle your mother-in-law's priceless crystal—with extreme caution—preferably while wearing gloves. There was a lot of wisdom embedded in that joke because a single fingerprint can start damage that might take years to become visible, but once it appears, that MS-65 Red cent might drop to MS-63 Red and Brown, taking thousands of dollars in value with it.

Skin chemistry affects copper cents dramatically even clean hands leave an invisible residue that can trigger spotting or toning patterns. While some collectors pride themselves on their "clean hands" technique, professional conservators consistently use cotton, latex, or nitrile gloves. The minimal cost and slight loss of tactile sensitivity represent cheap insurance against long-term damage.

Your workspace sets the stage for proper handling. A padded surface prevents accidental drops from becoming disasters. Proper lighting helps you position coins without awkward adjustments. Keep drinks and food away—that morning coffee splash could cost more than a year's collecting budget. Clean cotton pads or microfiber cloths provide safe resting places between examinations.

Master the rim-only hold. Support the coin's edge between thumb and forefinger, allowing full viewing while minimizing contact. When examining reverse details, roll the coin like a wheel rather than flipping it. This technique prevents pressure on design elements and reduces the risk of contact marks. For heavily worn pieces or cleaned coins, these precautions might seem excessive—but good habits protect your entire collection.

TOOLS FOR PROPER COIN MANIPULATION

That twisted pair of hardware store tweezers never should have touched a coin. I watched in horror as a new collector scraped his 1972 doubled die trying to remove it from a flip. The right tools might cost more initially, but they pay for themselves by preventing a single destructive moment.

Professional numismatic tools serve specific purposes: Precision tweezers feature smooth, curved tips designed to grip rims without marring surfaces. Quality pairs run $50-100, but their non-marking tips and precise tension control protect thousands in coin value. Avoid straight-tip tweezers—they can slip and scratch surfaces. The best pairs come from watchmaking suppliers who understand the need for precision.

Handling surfaces matter equally. A proper coin pad absorbs shock while providing contrast for viewing. The black velvet pad that came with your first collecting kit might look elegant, but its loose fibers can scratch copper surfaces. Investment-grade handling surfaces use specialized materials that combine protection with clarity:

- Premium suede pads with non-marking surfaces
- Microfiber mats designed specifically for numismatics
- Silicon-based surfaces that prevent sliding
- High-density foam padding beneath working areas
- Common mistakes often stem from impatience or overconfidence:
- Using household tweezers or pliers

- Grabbing coins from holders hastily
- Dropping coins directly onto hard surfaces
- Handling pieces right after eating or drinking
- Assuming clean hands eliminate need for tools
- Working without proper lighting
- Multitasking while examining valuable pieces

The most expensive tool in your kit should undoubtedly be your handling surface. A quality pad provides insurance against accidental drops, reduces eye strain through proper contrast, and maintains consistent viewing conditions. Consider it part of your grading equipment, not just protection.

STORAGE OPTIONS AND BEST PRACTICES

What starts as a temporary storage solution often becomes permanent by default. I recently examined a significant collection stored in 1980s PVC flips because the owner kept planning to "upgrade them next month." Those few dollars saved in proper storage turned into thousands in restoration costs. Today's storage decisions shape tomorrow's preservation reality.

Mylar Flips

Premium mylar flips represent the gold standard for individual coin storage. Their inert composition prevents chemical reactions with coin surfaces. The best examples use archival-grade materials tested for long-term stability. Look for flips that are marked "Museum Quality" or "Archival Safe"—these designations indicate materials free from harmful plasticizers. Double-pocket designs protect both sides while preventing coin movement.

Advantages:

- Chemical stability over decades
- Clear visibility for examination
- Protection against environmental contaminants
- Easy labeling for attribution details
- Stackable for efficient storage
- Reasonable cost per coin

Disadvantages:

- Require careful insertion technique
- May show wear at folds over time
- Premium versions cost more initially
- Can trap moisture if improperly sealed

Cardboard Holders

Modern cardboard holders have evolved far beyond their acidic ancestors. Today's archival-grade products use pH-neutral materials specifically designed for numismatic storage, however, they still present challenges for long-term copper storage:

Benefits:

- Excellent organization options
- Good visibility when new
- Traditional collecting aesthetic
- Lower initial cost
- Easy date recognition

Drawbacks:

- Even neutral cardboard can deteriorate
- Insertion slots may wear coins
- Limited protection from environment
- Difficulty monitoring coin surfaces
- Potential for hidden contamination

Plastic Storage Systems

The market offers numerous plastic storage options, but quality varies dramatically. Premium holders use inert polymers that remain stable over decades. Avoid anything containing PVC—it breaks down over time, leaving harmful residue on coin surfaces.

High-Grade Plastic Options:

- Polypropylene holders (stable, clear)
- Polyethylene containers (durable, protective)
- Acrylic capsules (excellent visibility)
- Premium storage boxes (environmental control)

Certified Holders

Third-party grading service holders provide superior protection but at a significant cost. Their sealed environments protect against environmental damage while providing tamper-evident security. Consider certification for:

- High-value errors
- Frequently handled pieces
- Investment-grade examples
- Important varieties

Each storage choice presents trade-offs between protection, visibility, cost, and convenience, what matters most though at the end of the day is matching your storage solutions to specific collecting goals while maintaining consistent quality standards across your collection.

8

THE MARKET FOR LINCOLN PENNY ERRORS

In 1995, a major doubled die discovery might take months to impact market prices. Today, social media can drive values within hours of the first photo posting. This instant information flow has revolutionized how error coins trade, creating both opportunities and challenges for collectors who understand market patterns.

Consider what happened when the 2016 "Naked Lincoln" die break surfaced. Within two hours of the first Facebook post, dealers were offering four-figure sums for example. By evening, price guides scrambled to establish baseline values. Within a week, the market had settled into defined price tiers based on break progression and grade. Twenty years ago, this price evolution would have taken months through traditional dealer networks and print publications.

This acceleration demands new collecting strategies. Waiting for printed price guides means missing opportunities. Modern error collectors need to understand both traditional market fundamentals and new digital dynamics. They must evaluate social media reports critically, distinguishing between genuine discoveries and misattributed varieties. The collector who can verify authenticity quickly often captures the best values.

Yet this rapid information flow carries risks. Rushed authentications lead to costly mistakes. Enthusiasm over new discoveries sometimes drives prices beyond sustainable levels. Understanding how to navigate these modern market forces while maintaining traditional collecting discipline has become crucial for success in error collecting.

CURRENT TRENDS IN THE ERROR COIN MARKET

The error coin market entered a new phase in 2021. Heritage Auctions' sale of a 1955 doubled die for $124,000 marked more than just a record price—it signaled heightened sophistication among collectors. Modern buyers demand both rarity and exceptional preservation. A decade ago, that same coin in the same grade might have brought half that amount.

Market dynamics show distinct patterns across error categories. Major doubled dies, particularly from the 1950s and 1960s, continue attracting premium prices regardless of market conditions. The 1969-S doubled die demonstrates this strength—even circulated examples consistently command five-figure prices. Meanwhile, more common varieties face increasing price pressure from certified populations that grow steadily as more examples surface.

Social media has transformed how error coins trade. Facebook groups dedicated to specific varieties share discoveries instantly. When a significant error surfaces, collectors debate authenticity in real-time, often reaching consensus before traditional attribution services weigh in. These platforms create immediate markets for new discoveries, sometimes establishing prices before dealers can gauge traditional market parameters.

Third-party grading services increasingly influence market direction. Their population reports provide crucial rarity data. When PCGS or NGC certifies a new variety, their attribution often becomes the market standard. Certification choices affect value—pieces in premium holders typically command 15-20% more than the same variety in basic holders.

Registry set competition drives demand for highest-grade examples. Collectors pursuing set completion often pay significant premiums for pieces that might upgrade their rankings. This competition particularly affects major varieties where few mint state examples exist. Some doubled dies show price spreads exceeding $10,000 between MS-64 and MS-65 grades.

The market increasingly rewards quality within rarity categories. Two 1972 doubled dies might share the same technical grade, but the piece showing stronger doubling characteristics often brings 25-30% more. This emphasis on visual impact affects everything from strike errors to die breaks, creating value hierarchies within individual variety categories.

PLACES TO SELL YOUR COINS

I know that selling decisions often prove more challenging than buying choices. What seems like a simple transaction actually involves numerous factors—market timing, buyer reach, fees, and payment security. A doubled die that might bring $3,000 at a coin show could yield $4,000 through an auction house, or $2,800 on eBay after fees. Understanding these dynamics helps maximize returns while minimizing risks.

Online Marketplaces

eBay dominates error coin transactions below $1,000. The platform's reach means quick sales when items are properly photographed and described. Yet success demands understanding the landscape. Professional images matter—dark, blurry photos typically yield 30% less than sharp, well-lit examples. Detailed descriptions mentioning specific variety attributions attract serious buyers. Top sellers maintain 99% feedback ratings while carefully documenting coin characteristics and shipping methods.

Heritage Auctions and Great Collections

These specialized platforms serve different market segments. Heritage excels with major rarities, particularly pieces above $2,500. Their marketing reach often produces record prices for significant errors. Great Collections bridges the gap between eBay and Heritage, proving particularly effective for certified errors in the $500-2,500 range. Both platforms provide superior photography and detailed descriptions, but their fees reflect these services.

Face-to-Face Sales at Shows

Major shows offer unique advantages for error sales. Buyers can examine pieces personally, often leading to faster decisions and stronger prices. The concentrated collector base means multiple bidders for quality pieces. Show sales eliminate shipping risks and payment delays. However, success requires understanding which attracts error specialists. The ANA World's Fair of Money typically yields better results than regional events.

Local Coin Shop Relationships

Building relationships with local dealers creates reliable sales channels. While they rarely pay auction-level prices, they offer immediate payment and zero fees. Smart collectors maintain connections with multiple dealers, understanding each one's specialties and buying patterns. Some dealers eagerly acquire minor varieties that prove troublesome to sell elsewhere.

Specialty Forums and Websites

CONECA's website and error-specific forums attract knowledgeable buyers. These venues excel for unusual varieties that mainstream collectors might overlook. Members often pay premium prices for well-documented new discoveries. Success requires building a reputation through accurate descriptions and fair pricing. Many significant errors find new homes through these specialized channels before reaching public auction.

Traditional Auction Houses

Major auction houses serve a crucial role for exceptional pieces. Their printed catalogs reach wealthy collectors who rarely attend shows. Commission rates typically range from 15-20%, but strong promotional efforts often yield record prices. Consider this option for:

- Major doubled dies above $5,000
- Previously undocumented varieties

- Historically significant pieces
- Exceptional condition rarities

TIPS FOR BUYING AND SELLING ONLINE

If you've ever been scammed, you'll know that the sting lasts far longer than the financial loss. Last year, a seemingly pristine 1969-S doubled die appeared on a popular auction site. The photos looked professional, the seller's feedback sparkled, and the price seemed fair at $12,000. Three collectors jumped at this "opportunity" before someone noticed the subtle tooling marks revealing a clever alteration. That incident taught the error community valuable lessons about online trading safeguards.

Digital markets create unique challenges for error coin trading. Authenticity verification depends entirely on photographs and seller descriptions. Wire transfers, once sent, rarely return. Even established sellers sometimes misattribute varieties or overlook crucial characteristics. Yet these same markets also offer unprecedented opportunities—instant access to global buyers, real-time price discovery, and efficient transaction processing.

You need both defensive skills and market knowledge so that you can accurately verify seller credentials, authenticate pieces through photos, and protect payment transactions has become as crucial as knowing variety attributions. This chapter explores proven strategies for safe and profitable online trading.

Creating Effective Listings

Professional listings don't happen by accident—you have to make them happen through careful preparation and attention to detail. When I see a doubled die listing with blurry photos and vague descriptions selling for half its potential value, I know the seller skipped crucial steps. The difference between a mediocre listing and one that attracts serious buyers often comes down to an extra hour of preparation.

Quality photography turns those average listings into compelling offerings. My most successful eBay sale—a 1972 doubled die that brought nearly $4,000—succeeded because I spent two hours capturing perfect images. Each photo revealed specific diagnostic points that serious buyers need to verify authenticity. The effort paid off through multiple bidders confidently pursuing a properly documented piece.

Photography Essentials

Proper lighting reveals doubled die characteristics that phone cameras often miss. Position two LED lights at 45-degree angles to eliminate shadows. Capture images against a neutral background—black for mint state pieces, and blue for circulated coins. Take multiple shots of crucial diagnostics:

- Complete obverse and reverse views
- Close-ups of major design elements
- Specific photos of error characteristics
- Edge details when relevant
- Any notable surface issues

Descriptions That Drive Sales

Technical accuracy matters more than marketing language. Make sure you include:

- Full variety attribution numbers
- Specific die stage characteristics
- Certification details if applicable
- Clear statements about surface quality
- Accurate grade assessments
- Known population data

Smart sellers document everything:

- When and where the coin was acquired
- Previous certification history
- Notable pedigree information
- Recent comparable sales
- Any restoration history
- Current market context

Pricing Strategy

Research recent sales of similar pieces. Consider these things:

- Current market trends

- Certification status
- Comparable transactions
- Population data
- Seasonal factors
- Condition rarity

Protection Policies

Each platform offers different safeguards:

- eBay's Money Back Guarantee
- PayPal's Seller Protection
- Platform-specific insurance options
- Shipping protection requirements
- Dispute resolution processes
- Return policies

Document every transaction step. Save all communications. Ship with tracking and insurance. These practices protect both buyer and seller while building market credibility.

Payment Methods and Shipping

Payment and shipping methods can make or break online transactions. Some time ago, a seller lost $2,800 on a doubled die when he accepted a cashier's check that turned out to be fraudulent. Meanwhile, his inadequate packaging allowed the coin to slide inside the envelope, creating hairlines that dropped the grade. Simple precautions could have prevented both disasters.

Payment Protocols

Each payment method carries specific risks and benefits: PayPal remains the safest option for both parties. Its seller protection covers documented transactions, while buyers gain purchase protection. Link PayPal accounts to specific bank accounts rather than debit cards for additional security. Always ship to verified PayPal addresses.

Wire transfers suit larger transactions but require extra verification:

Confirm bank details through multiple channels

- Document all communication
- Wait for full clearance before shipping
- Keep proof of all transaction details
- Consider escrow for five-figure sales

Shipping Strategy

Professional packaging prevents costly damage:

- Use heavy-duty flips inside rigid cardboard
- Double-box valuable pieces
- Include padding between layers
- Seal all edges with quality tape
- Consider signature confirmation
- Insure for full value

Common shipping mistakes include:

- Using regular envelopes for coins
- Inadequate padding around holders
- Visible descriptions of contents
- Insufficient insurance coverage
- Improper declaration of value
- Missing tracking options

Dispute Resolution

Document every step to prevent disputes:

- Photograph coins before shipping
- Save all packing materials
- Record serial numbers
- Keep shipping receipts
- Save all communications
- Maintain transaction records

When disputes arise:

- Respond promptly to all claims

- Provide clear documentation
- Follow platform guidelines
- Maintain professional tone
- Consider partial refunds
- Document resolution steps

Prevention proves cheaper than resolution. Clear policies, proper documentation, and professional shipping practices eliminate most potential disputes before they start.

Red Flags in Online Transactions

There are real-time opportunists out there watching for every chance to exploit eager collectors. Last month, within hours of a major doubled die discovery announcement, dozens of deceptive listings appeared online. Some showed artificially doubled coins. Others displayed stolen photos from legitimate sales. A few even offered "pre-orders" for pieces they didn't own. Only collectors who recognized these warning signs avoided costly mistakes.

Trust your instincts when details don't align:

Photos that seem recycled from other listings often mask counterfeit coins. Professional dealers take their own photos, and when images appear in multiple listings or show up in reverse image searches, assume the worst. Quality sellers document their specific pieces, not stock photos.

Price anomalies tell stories:

- Major varieties priced well below market
- "Buy It Now" options too good to refuse
- Urgent sales of valuable pieces
- Pressure to complete quick transactions
- Unusual payment method requirements
- Resistance to escrow suggestions

Seller behavior raises crucial flags:

- New accounts selling expensive errors
- Limited or obviously artificial feedback

- Unwillingness to provide additional photos
- Vague responses about coin history
- Pressure for off-platform transactions
- Excuses about certification costs

Watch for description red flags:

- Misused technical terms
- Incorrect attribution numbers
- Conflicting condition details
- Copy-pasted variety information
- Unclear progression photographs
- Missing crucial diagnostics

Even established sellers sometimes raise concerns:

- Sudden changes in selling patterns
- Unexpected specialty shifts
- Quality inconsistencies
- Communication style changes
- New payment requirements
- Unusual shipping methods

The strongest protection comes from developing systematic verification habits. Check every detail, especially when deals seem too perfect. Consider that professional dealers rarely miss major price opportunities—when something seems too good to be true, it usually tells you exactly what you need to know.

Building a Reputation as a Collector or Dealer

Small details make or break reputations in error collecting. Some time ago, a major auction house pulled a six-figure doubled die from their sale after a tiny repair became evident under magnification. The consignor's attempt to hide this minor flaw cost them both the sale and future consignment opportunities. Meanwhile, dealers who document even minor issues build client bases that last decades.

Accurate description builds long-term market credibility. Professional dealers know that every detail matters:

Surface Quality

Document every significant mark, even if seemingly minor:

- Location and severity of contact marks
- Toning patterns and color variations
- Signs of cleaning or restoration
- Evidence of environmental damage
- Strike characteristics and weakness
- Die state progression markers

Grade Assessment

Conservative grading protects your reputation:

- Compare against certified examples
- Note borderline characteristics
- Explain any grade-limiting factors
- Document lighting conditions used
- Reference specific grading standards
- Acknowledge subjective elements

Attribution Details

Precision in variety documentation matters:

- Specific die stage identification
- Known population information
- Previous certification history
- Attribution reference numbers
- Documented diagnostics
- Comparative characteristics

Market Context

Provide relevant background:

- Recent comparable sales
- Population changes

- Market trend information
- Condition rarity data
- Historical price patterns
- Known pedigree details

Bear in mind that today's minor omission becomes tomorrow's major dispute. Building a reputation for meticulous accuracy pays dividends through repeat business and referrals. The error coin market particularly rewards sellers known for detailed, honest descriptions.

Sharing Knowledge and Contributing to the Community

Building a knowledgeable collecting community requires patience and generosity. At a recent show, I watched a veteran dealer spend an hour explaining die characteristics to a teenager who'd brought in a box of machine-doubled cents. That investment in education created another careful observer who now helps spot genuine varieties. Meaningful contribution also takes many forms. Some collectors document new die stages, photographing progression changes that help others understand variety development. Others maintain detailed population data, tracking appearances of significant errors across different market venues. Even sharing basic authentication tips helps prevent costly mistakes within the community.

Online forums benefit from careful, accurate posting:

- Document new variety discoveries thoroughly
- Share high-quality diagnostic photos
- Provide detailed attribution information
- Offer constructive authentication feedback
- Maintain professional discussion tone
- Address misconceptions respectfully

Local coin clubs need active participants:

- Present educational programs
- Mentor newer collectors
- Share reference materials
- Host attribution workshops

- Provide market updates
- Support club activities

Publication contributions advance error knowledge:
- Submit articles to specialty journals
- Document new discoveries
- Share research findings
- Update variety listings
- Report market trends

Today's beginner might discover tomorrow's major variety; every collector who learns proper attribution techniques becomes another set of eyes scanning for significant errors. This knowledge network is what strengthens our hobby while protecting its participants from costly mistakes.

Handling Disputes Properly

Every now and again, even meticulously planned transactions encounter unexpected problems. A doubled die arrives with a hairline crack in the slab—invisible in pre-shipping photos but clear upon delivery. A certified mint error shows signs of cleaning not disclosed in the listing. A priority mail package takes an unexplained detour through three states. These moments test both buyer and seller, revealing character through response rather than circumstance.

Professional dispute resolution requires a systematic approach. Start by acknowledging the issue without admitting fault. Document everything—photograph damage, save all communications, and verify shipping records. Many conflicts resolve themselves when both parties focus on evidence rather than emotion.

Clear communication makes the difference:
- Respond promptly to all messages
- Keep emotions out of replies
- Focus on specific issues
- Propose reasonable solutions
- Document all agreements
- Follow through consistently

Smart sellers anticipate common disputes:

- Grade disagreements
- Shipping damage claims
- Attribution questions
- Condition disputes
- Delivery delays
- Payment issues

The strongest resolution often comes from offering choices rather than single solutions. When that slab arrived damaged, I gave the buyer three options: full refund upon return, partial refund while keeping the coin, or re-slabbing at my expense. This approach lets buyers participate in resolution while maintaining professional standards. Today's dispute resolution affects tomorrow's business opportunities. Collectors talk to each other, your handling of one problem influences dozens of potential future transactions. Professional conduct during conflicts builds market reputation more effectively than smooth sales.

CONCLUSION

Success is born from patience and knowledge, but it also stems from something deeper—the thrill of discovery. That moment when the light catches a coin just right, revealing an unnoticed doubled die. The surge of excitement when you spot a major die break hidden in a dealer's bargain bin. These discoveries still happen every day, even in our well-documented era.

The tools for success already exist. Reference materials document known varieties. Digital photography reveals diagnostic points. Professional certification provides authentication. Yet the most valuable tool remains consistent study—learning the subtle indicators that separate genuine errors from alterations, significant varieties from minor ones.

Every significant error collection started with a single piece and a decision to learn more. Understanding how these pieces were created, what makes them valuable, and how to authenticate them transforms collecting from speculation to expertise. This knowledge builds confidence while protecting against costly mistakes.

The error coin market rewards prepared collectors, but it rewards passionate ones even more. Those moments spent examining coins under proper lighting, researching die characteristics, and learning from experienced collectors pay off in both knowledge and value. Every new discovery adds another chapter to the ongoing story of mint production, and your next significant find might be just one coin away.

The best collections tell two stories—one about the coins themselves, and one about the collector who took the time to understand them. Which story will your collection tell?

REFERENCES

A look at mint errors and their value to rare coin collectors. (2015, February 2). Rare Coin Investments. https://rarecoins.co.za/a-look-at-mint-errors-and-their-value-to-rare-coin-collectors/

Admin. (2022, November 9). *Your guide to collecting Lincoln pennies.* Lccoins. https://www.lccoins.com/default/blog/post/your-guide-to-collecting-lincoln-pennies

Coin dealer that buys rare mint error coins. (2015, January 3). A&D Coin and Jewelry Exchange. https://adcoinandjewelry.com/coins/mint-errors-mistakes/

Coin grading explained. (n.d.). Rare Coin Investments. https://rarecoins.co.za/coin-grading-explained/

Collecting the Lincoln Penny 101. (2023, January 23). Coinagemag.com; COINage Magazine. https://www.coinagemag.com/collecting-the-lincoln-penny-101/

Collector's guide to error coins. (2024, July 11). Intelligent Collector. https://intelligentcollector.com/collectors-guide-to-error-coins/

G, T. (2021, September 15). *Strategies for building a coin collection.* Buy & Sell Gold & Silver Wisely in Denver, CO . https://rmcoin.com/blog/strategies-for-building-a-coin-collection-rocky-mountain-coin/.

Grading Lincoln cents. (2024). Ngccoin.com; NGC. https://www.ngccoin.com/coin-grading-guide/grading-lincoln-cents/

How to determine the value of a mint error coin. (2023, March 15). PCGS. https://www.pcgs.com/news/how-to-determine-the-value-of-a-mint-error-coin

Kierstin S. (2014, December 3). *Starting a coin collection.* Littleton Coin Blog. https://blog.littletoncoin.com/3-easy-steps-starting-a-coin-collection/

Lincoln cent grading guide. (2024). Lincolncent Forum. https://www.lincolncentforum.com/lincoln-cent-grading-guide/

Lincoln Cents (1909-Date). (2009, July 22). Complete Coin Guide. https://lincolncents.net/

Lincoln head cents collection. (2024). Littleton Coin Company. https://www.littletoncoin.com/shop/Lincoln-Head-Cents-Collection?srsltid=AfmBOoqtfxz8vZfPzIwX7pGiImWBuhRzvKV-dGfj8rN3pCROxigEBQ__

McMorrow-Hernandez, J. (2020, November 24). *What are the different penny errors and how much are they worth?* Gainesvillecoins.com; Gainesville Coins. https://www.gainesvillecoins.com/blog/lincoln-penny-errors?srsltid=AfmBOortmw7sua_fB_FX-T56NftK-gxyX8s4-zsG25mzidBF9KflHjAD

Penny. U.S. Mint for kids. (2024, May 2). United States Mint. https://kids.usmint.gov/learn/kids/about-the-mint/penny

Ten amazing rare lincoln cents worth a lot of money. (2024, July 31). CoinWeek: Rare Coin, Currency, and Bullion News for Collectors. https://coinweek.com/ten-amazing-lincoln-cents-worth-money/

Timeline Tuesday: Lincoln Penny - Nebraska state historical society. (2022, October 29). Nebraska State Historical Society. https://history.nebraska.gov/timeline-tuesday-lincoln-penny/

Valuable Lincoln pennies: Mint marks & coins worth money. (2024, October 26). Accurate Precious Metals. https://accuratepmr.com/blog/valuable-lincoln-pennies-mint-marks-coins-worth-money/?srsltid=AfmBOopkt3Zcr0Sj1QxkEfQgSQFOhhwvhL2YC-SismPM6xztFyn5-i9O

What you might not know about Lincoln pennies. (n.d.). The Spruce Crafts. https://www.thesprucecrafts.com/history-of-the-lincoln-cent-768785

Made in the USA
Columbia, SC
23 July 2025

60962886R00061